D0353662

THE JACARANDA CHILDREN
Margaret Mamaki

HARMATTAN PRESS

2004

Publisher	Harmattan Press P.O. Box 277, CT10 1WT UK
Support Publisher	Pontefract Press 17 Linden Terrace Pontefract WF8 4AE pontefractpress1@btinternet.com
Writer	Margaret Mamaki
Editor	Brian Lewis
Design	Jacob Schühle Lewis
Support	Reini Schühle and Margret Morton
Printer	Aeroprinting, Jarrow, NE32 3EF
ISBN	1 900325 40 3

I have related events that took place over forty years. At times my memory may have lapsed so any shortcomings are regretted. Many names have been changed in the script to avoid embarrassment. Everything that has been written is my own responsibility. If I have offended, it is unintentional.

Margaret Mamaki

TO ELI, MY HUSBAND AND BEST FRIEND
AND TO THE JACARANDA CHILDREN

M y thanks to the many persons who have helped me to write this book: To Maggie Solley my first tutor who started me off in writing; to all my good friends in the Biscuit Club especially Liz; to Joy Voisey; to Pat Howard; always steadfast, whose sound advice and experience is greatly valued.

A very special appreciation to my writing guru - Brian Lewis for his hours of time, generosity and encouragement especially in those times when I faltered and wanted to give up; to Jacob Schühle-Lewis who designed the cover and to Reini Schühle for all her support.

To my children, Caroline, Andrew and especially Joe for their encouragement. Most importantly, to my husband Eli, who listened and gave positive advice.

PROLOGUE

Three days before Christmas in 1961, the Aureole sailed from foggy Liverpool. On board was a young family. Eli, a newly qualified doctor, was returning to his homeland, Nigeria, with his young wife, Margaret, and two infant children. He had been studying medicine in Britain for seven years.

Their ship berthed in Lagos and they travelled six hundred miles north to Kaduna where Eli eventually started a clinic right inside the busy part of the town. After a few years they were able to build their dream family house. Later they bought some farmland outside the town where they planted orchards and set up a restaurant and pottery. The farm was called the Jacaranda. Whilst Eli ran his clinic in town, Margaret spent her time working at the Jacaranda. This is her story.

JACARANDA
21 February 2000

I was marooned 22 kilometres from home at the Jacaranda. Oily smoke blotted out the sun. Distant explosions forced bursts of flame high into the sky. Some of our workers stood around in groups. I could hear them talking. One was gesticulating wildly, beating his fists against his head. Voices were raised and their dazed faces portrayed incredulity and horror. I stared in disbelief and gradually became aware of the terror that engulfed Kaduna.

The cook, a Maiduguri man, came over to me. 'I'm going to risk it and go back to town. My wife's just had a baby. I have six kids. Oh God! I don't know if they're still alive. In any case she'll be worried out of her mind.' He was an old member of staff - sweat was running down his forehead, a general panic was building up.

Earlier that day, we had been told of rioting and bloodshed in street battles raging all over Kaduna. Some of the junior staff piled into the minibus. They were mainly Efiks and Idomas and were speaking in their languages. I'd already warned them not to try to leave but their grim faces were set stubbornly. One waiter looked at me and with a pleading voice, spoke. 'Make you no stop us, we de go for home.'

I had foreseen this possibility and already removed the keys. 'You'll be killed if you move beyond these gates. You heard what your driver said - the road is littered with bodies. The rioters are slaughtering anyone they see. If your families have survived, they'll need you alive not dead.' My firmness produced a response but inwardly I felt drained and didn't know where to turn to control the panic that was once again welling up all around.

Throughout that day, I'd been in radio contact with my husband at our house. He warned me to stay at Jacaranda because the situation around him was deteriorating. Moslems and Christians were fighting in the streets over the implementation of Sharia law. Mobs were gathering and hurling missiles at our roof. I was isolated at the farm, cut off and powerless to render help.

Mohammed, one of our potters, and a few Tuareg guards were standing in a separate group. They were the only Moslems, well outnumbered by the Christian staff. They looked scared though Mohammed clutched an ancient dane-gun in an attempt to exhibit courage.

I summoned the groups and appealed to them. 'We're all in this mess. We've worked together peacefully all these years. I know we're of different religions, but we mustn't fight amongst ourselves. There is one God and I suggest that you all go and pray silently for your loved ones.'

At that moment Yisa, our shop assistant came running towards me. 'Doctor is calling on the radio. He says terrible things are happening over there and he wants to talk to you now.'

I rushed to the round house where the short wave radio was housed. Grasping the hand set, I pressed the button and spoke. 'This is Mamajac, can you hear me?'

There was a slight pause and then I heard Eli's clear voice, 'I'm hearing you loud and clear. I'm still in the main house and completely surrounded by a mob. Hundreds of Moslem youths are attacking our compound. Our roof is burning and our cars and gas cylinders have been torched. Many of our workers are imprisoned with me here in the house. Their wives and children are screaming in terror. Both our bungalows next door are in flames. I've used all my cartridges.'

A deep sigh followed, and then, 'My darling, I can do no more, this is to say good-bye.' Our conversation ended abruptly. I called him back, over and over again, but it seemed as if the radio had been switched off.

The workers looked at me sympathetically. 'Sorry ma.'

At first I hadn't been able to grasp the full implication of this message, but gradually the truth dawned. Our house had been under attack since midday, and it was now dark. I heard a buzzing in my ears. As this faintness faded, utter despair followed.

I walked outside into a dark stillness, only interrupted by the sounds of frogs, crickets and nightjars. How could I go on living if my husband were burnt alive, the mental torture would be too much to bear. I'd already witnessed the horrendous death of a youth murdered by a burning tyre-necklace, a sickening experience that had haunted me ever since. I had been told earlier that day that a burning tyre had been hung on the gate of our house in town. I did not cry and scream for that wouldn't help.

It was then that I noticed Bello, a graduate potter I'd brought up and educated. He was now an adult and a double amputee since the age of seven. We had always been close. He was a Moslem and I'd encouraged him to stick to his religion, knowing that it was a strong part of his culture and family tradition. Now his head was buried in his shirt to hide his tears. I grasped the handles of his wheelchair and pushed him into the enclosed garden. We stayed there among the ferns and lilies in silent meditation. I prayed that my precious husband would be saved, and that if he were to die, his end would be swift and painless.

Time stood still as the night breeze wafted over my face

and the branches of the trees swayed above us. The brightness of the stars was only interrupted to the north by the glow of distant fires. Standing there with Bello, an inner peace seemed to settle on me, an unaccountable calmness. I wondered about this strange feeling. What did it mean? Was it over? What had happened to my husband? Was he dead or alive?

As if he read my thoughts, Bello shifted in his chair, 'Let's go and find out if there's any news.'

As we walked towards the thatched office, Yisa came running towards us looking excited. 'I've just heard another radio message. Umaru just called from the main office back in town. He said he saw lorry loads of riot police drive into your compound. They've been shooting at the mob that has now dispersed.'

I grabbed the radio set and shouted, 'Umaru, tell me, is my husband still alive?'

A hesitant voice came from the other end: 'That's what we are trying to find out. I've been phoning the staff in the main house, but they are not picking up. I was right there in that mob close to your house when I saw the riot police arrive. I had to run for my life because they started shooting at us. There's a curfew and it is too dangerous to go out there again.'

I knew that Umaru was speaking from the restaurant's main office, just a mile from our house, so I stayed close to the radio waiting for another message to come through. At last he called: 'Ogbaje phoned. Doctor is alive and he's coming to rescue you.' Umaru was one of our most steadfast workers.

My initial feeling of relief was soon changed. I knew that Eli's route to Jacaranda would be through densely populated suburbs, industrial estates and shanty towns. From what I had heard, they were in flames. I had to prevent him from risking his life. 'Tell doctor to stay in town and find a safe place for the night. He must be exhausted. He shouldn't worry about me - but why can't I speak to him? Is his radio dead?'

A firm response came from the other end. 'Ogbaje said that he's already left the house. The riot police are escorting him.' I suddenly felt very thirsty. I realised I hadn't eaten all day. My trousers and shirt seemed glued to my body and my legs were shaking.

Radio reports had described the mayhem that was taking place all over Kaduna. How would Eli survive, travelling along a road blocked by mobs of youths, probably drugged up to their eyeballs and completely out of control? Why was he attempting this journey for my sake? I wasn't in any danger. I wondered about his mental state. How could a man of seventy survive such a violent attack? Our house had been under siege for seven and a half hours. I longed to be with him, to hug and comfort him. I looked at my watch. It was 9 pm.

For the next hour I listened for the sound of a vehicle that would bring Eli to me. I pushed the farm gates open and walked bare-footed down the laterite driveway towards the road. Stepping onto the tarmac I noticed that it still felt warm from the heat of that torturous day. Knowing that a curfew had been imposed, to venture outside the gates was probably reckless, but by now I was completely irrational. Walking up and down that dark road, I thought about the warnings that earlier in the day had seemed so insignificant.

That same morning, I'd jumped out of bed before daybreak, enthusiastic about the workshop I was to organize for teachers. I had needed an early start.

As I left the house, Eli warned me, 'The Christians are going to march to Government House today with a letter of protest against Sharia Law. There are bound to be some counter demonstrations from the Moslems. You must be careful along the road.' This was bad news. I knew that peace was impossible when religious fanatics from both sides gather en masse; the atmosphere would be volatile if not explosive.

As an English woman married to a Nigerian for over forty years, I did not believe that I was under any threat, but our town house was vulnerable as it was situated in a predominantly Moslem area of Kaduna. I feared for Eli because rioting Moslems had threatened him before. The mosque along the road from our house was a hotbed of fanaticism where jobless youths might take advantage of any situation to cause trouble. They used to sit on the culvert outside our gate smoking hemp and selling jerry cans of black-market petrol. They were a wild lot and whenever the police raided the area, they would hide in the mosque. Their habitual brawling often startled us during the night, setting off all the dogs in the neighbourhood.

Although Eli and I were born Christians, we didn't often go to church. I could understand why this riot had happened. In recent years life for the masses had become full of hardship – many turned to religion as their only hope. There were many sincere believers, both Christian and Moslem. The elite society flourished at the expense of the poor.

I spent my days out at the Jacaranda, where I ran a pottery. The noticeably high rate of infant mortality in the villages had shocked me, so in the late 1980s I had started a voluntary organisation and named it 'Hope for the Village Child'. With a small team of nurses and voluntary helpers, I was trying to provide the children around Jacaranda with primary healthcare, schools and clean water. The work was fulfilling and I had felt contented with this new way of life.

As I stood in the road, my thoughts wandered over the four decades we'd lived in Kaduna. Why should we have been so brutally attacked? As far as I knew we had no enemies. My husband was a medical practitioner who'd insisted on working close to the market where most of his patients lived. They were poor people, of all creeds and cultures. His kindness had often over-ruled his business sense and it was said that he didn't know how to live as a Nigerian because he refused to pay bribes. Many of his patients had no hope of ever settling their medical fees, but he would help them out. He'd spent much of his spare time trying to set up a school for deaf children and had always resisted being dragged into politics. He loved playing golf but most of his leisure time was spent growing fruits and creating a beautiful garden at home and at our farm. A loving, contemplative man, he would frequently come to breakfast smiling gently, and present me with a fragrant rose. In his autumn years he'd become quieter, devoting his time to reading Eastern philosophy. He spent hours with his patients, always trying to heal them by counselling and by offering simple alternative methods rather than by pushing tranquillisers. Why had this mob attacked him? Jealousy? Surely people could see we were struggling to keep financially afloat in this turbulent time.

During that wait, uncertain if I would ever see Eli again, I thought of the home he'd created so lovingly. When we'd started to plant our land and build the house, it had just been an empty patch of earth, grazed by Fulani cattle, next to a small settlement of thatched houses. Over the years the neighbourhood had expanded into a dense settlement of low cost houses and shacks. Mosques had gradually sprung up around us and the road outside had become congested with traffic. Later a petrol station had been built on the opposite corner of the road.

In spite of the noise and petrol fumes, our garden had become a retreat, an oasis set in the confused world. We had planted teak trees and palms to shield us from the noise, and they now towered like monuments under the glaring sun. Vines twisted around their massive trunks. Golden Shower blossoms hung profusely, creating an orange iridescent waterfall. Ferns, orchids and leafy creepers grew all over these palms; their struggle to dominate, spread and climb towards the sky created a tiny jungle full of creatures. Sunbirds hovered, wings vibrating, dipping their long beaks into the orchids. Beyond an iron gate was a shady courtyard where there was a small pond and a fountain. Standing there you could see bright red goldfish, the type that have telescopic eyes. Purple and cream water lilies covered the surface of the water. These waxy flowers were the armchairs for hundreds of tiny frogs. In our house garden there was always an intoxicating scent of flowers, especially wild jasmine. It was this, our paradise that had just been raped. Rumbling in the distance told me that vehicles were approaching. Hastily I made my way back through the gates.

A duck-egg blue Peugeot, which I recognised, rattled into the farm. Behind it was a huge combat lorry and on the deck, sub-machine guns poised, were about twelve riot police. Two heavily armed police emerged from the Peugeot, followed by Gideon, my husband's in-law. He was frowning and shook his head in exhaustion. Last of all came Eli. I hardly recognized him as the man I'd breakfasted with earlier that day. His usual calm demeanour had changed and he was sobbing.

I hugged him, regardless of the crowd of staff who'd gathered to find out what was happening. They all stared at us. His shaking would not cease. It seemed as if the torment of what he had experienced had broken his spirit. I whispered in his ear, 'Don't grieve. It must have been a terrible ordeal but it's over and you're alive.'

'Why did they do this to me? What had I done to make them attack me?' In shock he blurted out fragments, telling of his ordeal and then a story that he told and retold. It was as if in the telling, he sought sense for his ghastly experience. I heard how a mob of youths had attacked our house with stones and burning bottles of petrol. How the women and children had run for shelter in the main house, screaming in terror. Over thirty people had been caught up inside our house when it was set alight. He explained how in desperation he had used his shotgun in self-defence. He thought he had hit a flame bearer. At the height of the attack Mrs Ogbaje, our cook's wife, had collapsed with a heart attack. Dizzy with pain he had defended the house. A few Moslem staff trapped with him had tried to call the commissioner of police who kept promising that help was on its way. Numerous friends had telephoned to find out exactly what was happening and had promised to arrange for rescuers to be sent. There were terrifying explosions as our cars, gas cylinders and generator were destroyed. With every explosion, the crowd had whooped with delight. Eli was tormented by the trauma and lost control of his emotions. John, our senior healthworker, patted his back and led him aside, trying to calm him. Some of the crowd followed. They gathered round, sympathising and listening.

I had to decide what to do. I asked Gideon, 'Where did these riot police come from?'

17

'Can you believe it? They came from Zamfara State, it's a hundred and fifty kilometres away and it took them over four hours to find our house.'

I turned to their chief, a serious man in full battle-dress, hand grenades hanging on his belt. 'Who sent you?'

'Don't you worry, my boss sent me.'

I turned to Gideon, 'Do you know who sent him?'

Gideon shrugged and replied, 'He won't say but it must have been somebody high up. We had contacted so many friends who'd promised to help us, but I don't know who actually sent these police.'

I looked at Gideon's battered old Peugeot and noticed that the plastic lights were burnt. 'Why did you use your car? It's hardly roadworthy - couldn't you have used something more reliable?'

He frowned. 'No, every single vehicle in our compound was torched.'

Remembering the precious Suzuki Jeep, used to convey sick children to hospital, I gasped. 'Surely not our project jeep?'

Gideon nodded sadly. Although the Suzuki was the least valuable of the vehicles burnt, this shock was like a whiplash. The hoodlums who used to sit by our gate knew of the sick and disabled children that were carried to hospital every week in that jeep. How could they be so wicked? He sighed, 'Even the school desks you were given by Unicef went up in flames together with our ambulance.'

The extent of this massive destruction was slowly dawning on me. 'Why didn't your car get burnt?'

Gideon smiled. 'They tried, but it wouldn't burn; each time they lit it with petrol the fire went out.'

I chuckled, knowing him to be a devout and sincere

Christian. 'You see! Your prayers worked!'

I was pleased to see his smile, but inwardly wondered if it had been his prayers or the thick mud that coated the chassis. Then somewhat chastened I realised how brave Gideon had been to drive out to Jacaranda that night. He still maintained his calmness and I believe that his deep faith was helping him.

'Weren't you terrified?' I asked

'Yes, I thought we were all finished. We saw the mob hacking Christians to death with machetes. Even after they were dead, they went on hacking at the bodies like crazy people.'

'Did Eli really have to shoot?'

'Oh yes. Some men had come through the broken gate carrying flaming torches. Our roof was already on fire and most of the cars had been set alight; they were determined to burn the ambulance. We feared they were going to burn us alive in the main house. After those shots, there was an ominous silence followed by a lull from the mob. Then, the Imam started calling for prayers. After the prayers, the attack became more ferocious than ever. Only God spared our lives. It was a miracle that these police came when they did. We were almost finished.'

Eli seemed overwrought beyond all human endurance. 'I've preserved life all these years, why did they attack me?' I wondered if he would ever recover from the trauma.

The commanding officer interrupted our anguished discussion. 'Where do you want to sleep this night? Where shall we take you?'

To my dismay Eli replied 'Back to our house.'

I grabbed his arm, protesting, 'That's a crazy risk - haven't you been through enough? We are safe here and the village people will protect us.'

But Eli was adamant. 'We must leave Kaduna today. After the hatred and destruction I've witnessed, I never ever want to return. I want to get away from this town and this country now. The problem is that our passports are locked in our safe. We'll have to go back for them.'

The riot police were muttering in the background, as if they had a problem. I wondered about their religion because I knew that Zamfara was predominantly Moslem and had been the first state to adopt Sharia Law. In many ways I distrusted them but inner reasoning controlled negative thoughts. I recollected that these police had been the ones to rescue Eli.

A young corporal approached and saluted the commanding officer. 'We need diesel for the truck. The tank is empty.'

I remembered that the farm generator had recently been filled. Two farm labourers were given instructions and hastily disappeared into the dark, armed with a rubber tube and a bucket. It was not the first time that they had tapped our generator for diesel. Once the lorry had been fed, we were ready to leave Jacaranda. We braced ourselves for the journey back to town and to our violated home. The remaining workers bade us a safe journey. I knew that they would not be in any danger, so remote from town.

I found myself wedged in the back of Gideon's spring-less Peugeot. On my left a riot policeman who aimed his automatic rifle through the broken car window, on my right Eli, a broken man. In the front seat was another policeman who stuck his gun out of the opposite window. Gideon was driving carefully and trying hard to concentrate. He was a plump, kindly man, prone to high blood pressure, but tonight he remained totally calm. Behind followed the huge combat lorry with riot police ready to shoot. Although it was dark, the truck overshadowed us menacingly.

Our small procession drove through the countryside towards the red glow. On the way we passed smouldering tyres, shattered glass and burnt out cars. I recognized the Pathfinder that I'd used earlier that morning to drive to Jacaranda. Its windscreen was smashed but I dared not ask Gideon to stop. Our two drivers, Sylvester and Tony had promised that they would keep away from the town. They had earlier persuaded me to let them go to rescue their children who were trapped in our house. They thought they could drive through the bush to the riverbank and walk across the dry riverbed to our house. It seemed they hadn't made it and I wondered if they were still alive. None of us spoke a word because we were staring at the destruction along the route. Charred bodies lay burning in the tarmac.

Some soldiers jumped off the lorry and dragged them aside. I heard one say, 'This one's still breathing.' There was a terrible stench of burnt flesh and the unmistakable smell of blood. There was junk everywhere, broken cement blocks, tree trunks, burning oil, lumps of metal. For a time, the road was completely blocked and we were forced to wait while the police tried to clear a passage through the rubble. A few youths ventured out from houses lining the route and the police on the lorry fired their automatics straight at them. The noise was deafening. I protested. 'They're only children. Don't shoot them.'

The policeman rasped back 'There's a curfew. We're ordered to shoot.'

We moved forward into Sabon Tasha, the tanker village

where the red glow we'd seen from the Jacaranda glared like molten lava. Everything there was burning, even in the depths of this shanty town. We were surrounded by fire and I could hear agonised crying. This was the village where huge tankers would line up before going into the refinery to load oil. Now some were straddled across our path, as if their drivers had tried to escape from the terror, only to be caught. Smouldering tyres forced Gideon to squeeze his Peugeot close to these burning wrecks. The heat was overpowering and I wondered if their fuel tanks had already exploded. I knew that we were in terrible danger.

Eli said, 'Margaret, don't look.' But I continued to stare at the horror being unveiled. There was a burnt-out bus - its passengers had been roasted. Their arms hung outside the broken windows, twisted as if they had been clutching at something whilst the fire consumed them.

I felt very strange, as if I was no longer there. I felt like a bird, hovering above the devastation and free from danger. I started to feel light-headed - detached from what was taking place. I questioned why I was still alive. The loss of all feeling was a relief because I was no longer afraid. I continued to gaze out of the window unmoved by the terrible scenes, whilst the soldiers continued to shoot at any being that had broken the night curfew. Part of me was dead.

***

I had left Bello with the other workers. I knew he was in no immediate danger, sheltered back at the Jacaranda, away from the carnage. But I still felt a deep sadness, as I reflected back over the years I had known him. Would I ever see him again?

It had been a breezy harmattan morning, back in the

sixties when Thomas Kilba, our elderly cook, called me to come to the back door. He pointed towards a concrete slab normally used for smashing coconuts open and for butchering meat. There, propped on the hard surface was a pale blue bundle - its shape was rather odd. I stared at it and noticed that it had a face. A stern Hausa man stood nearby. He had a white beard and a turban showing that he'd recently returned from Mecca. He also smelt of the spicy perfume sold in Jeddah. I recognized him as the cook for some friends who'd left Nigeria. He was talking to our guard and seemed to be full of anger. Undaunted, and out of curiosity, I approached, 'Good morning, what brings you here?'

He was chewing and his teeth were stained a rusty colour from Kola-nuts. He pointed to the child. The words that came from his mouth were shocking. 'It would have been better if the Almighty Allah had taken him altogether instead of removing half of him!'

I stared at the boy who, to my amazement, smiled back at me. I looked closer and realized that he had no legs. He was balancing on his torso, like a skittle. He must have been about seven.

I wondered if he could speak. 'What's your name?' The child didn't reply, but his smile broadened. I repeated, this time in Hausa, 'Menene sunan ka?'

To my delight his clear voice replied, 'Bello.'

The father's callous words had infuriated me, so I challenged him. 'Would you be as cheerful if both your legs had been cut off? Look at his smile, it's a gift from God.'

The man jerked his head and his anger seemed to change to despair. 'What can I do with him? I have many children. He'll become a beggar.'

The child's rounded face with the softest brown eyes gazed up at me and smiled. I studied the curly eyelashes, reasoned for a moment and then melted. 'He hasn't lost his brain; we must try to give him the best education possible. Would you allow me to help him?'

The miserable man nodded, 'You can have him. What use is he to me like this?'

I studied the deep tribal marks cut in the man's face. I felt uneasy about him so replied cautiously, 'I could give him some lessons to prepare him for school.'

His bitterness exceeded his manners. He waved his hand in the boy's direction, 'Do what you like with him.'

At that moment a wailing call for prayer sounded from a nearby mosque. Hastily he gathered the boy up, rolled up his prayer mat, then sauntered away towards the mosque.

The next morning I drove to the Red Cross headquarters and bought a tricycle specially designed for the disabled. It had been knocked together from old Raleigh bicycles - its handlebars were attached to some pedals and a chain. It seemed perfect but it would not fit into my car so Buba our gardener rode it proudly back to the house, waving and greeting all his friends along the road as if he were driving a brand-new Mercedes Benz.

The news of the new tricycle spread throughout the village and must have reached Bello's family because his elder brother carried him to our house. When Bello saw the tricycle he didn't waste a moment but propelled himself towards it, using his arms like oars. He almost flew through the air as he bounced onto the seat. Then he took off, arms rotating like the paddles of a windmill, faster and faster, round the driveway. Eventually exhausted, he stopped. Tears were running down his cheeks that were almost bursting with smiles.

That was the start of a journey we shared together, to school and eventually through university. I could never have foreseen the frustrations. The road was uphill and we journeyed over some thorny ground and jagged stones.

Brilliant exam results were 'mislaid' and applications to university were 'accidentally' lost. Forgetting the God they worshipped so noisily, the overdressed elite were always waiting to slide their sons' applications in through the backdoor, only too willing to pay the 'fee' demanded by a hungry clerk in control of admission lists. To them, a legless boy in a wheelchair from a humble background was unimportant. Why should he be entitled to a place in secondary school or university? Traditionally he was destined to become a beggar.

I did not see Bello's father again from the day he left our house. Bello eventually graduated with an upper second-class degree from Ahmadu Bello University, Zaria.

***

I thought of him as we went on that road, but remember very little of the remainder of the journey to our house except that as we rounded the bend, gunfire rang out and the crowds rapidly dispersed into the mosque along the road. We had reached home.

Jagged holes gaped through the high wall. The smashed gate hung limp, attached by one dislocated hinge. On it was hooked the wire skeleton of the tyre that had been meant for my husband's neck. We drove into the garden. There was a stench of petrol fumes and smoke. The sinister silence was that of a dead planet. I stumbled over a piece of charred wood, and became aware of stones, broken glass and rubble littering the ground that looked like a war zone.

The flame trees and palms still glowed red from the fire. They had faithfully shielded our house from the missiles, but with expensive consequence. The creepers and blossoms were gone, consumed by the flames. I wondered if the tiny tree creatures had escaped. Entering the courtyard, I noticed the pond was half empty - water lilies uprooted. A thick film of petrol floated on the water, shrouding hundreds of dead fish. One of our faithful dogs lay dead beside the pond, his fur singed from his body. I had to control my emotions by remembering that humans and babies had also been torched. At that moment a sudden breeze wafted the charred palm fronds, and tiny, coiled shreds fell all around us. It was as if the trees were weeping.

Ogbaje's daughter Lucy cautiously opened our front door. Our large sitting room was dark and at first I could only smell the stench of sweat. As my eyes became accustomed to the darkness I saw that the marble floor was covered with sleeping women and children. My driver's wife, Ada, struggled to sit up. Her toddler seemed to be having a nightmare and shrieked intermittently. 'Welcome Ma. Thank God that you're still alive. Your man has saved our lives. Without his courage we would all be dead.'

The study door opened and Ogbaje, our cook-steward, came out. He still maintained his quiet dignity.

'I'm so sorry to hear of your wife's heart attack, is she feeling better now?'

He nodded in gratitude: 'The injection doctor gave must have saved her life. We thought she was finished. We thank God for what master did for us all. We would have been killed. Madam, you must leave quickly before it is too late. The mob will return after curfew. They are still after doctor and they seem determined to kill him.'

'But why should they be hunting him? Aren't they after Christians generally? Why should they target him?' Ogbaje shook his head and replied, 'From what we witnessed today, he must have been on their list.'

I recoiled. There was no time to be lost. Miraculously our telephone was still working and, as we had arranged, Eli made some telephone calls to seek shelter for us, whilst Lucy guided me upstairs to our bedroom. At the top of the stairs, I could see stars shining through a huge hole in our still smouldering roof. The door to our guest wing was closed.

'Don't open it,' Lucy cautioned me 'there is still fire in there.'

The smoke was thick but a cool breeze streamed through the passage window where the glass had been shattered. I was wading through water and fragments of glass towards our bedroom wing when I noticed blood all over the floor. 'What happened here?'

Lucy held a small candle and peered at the floor. 'My dad was injured by the broken glass. He was running to call for doctor to help after my mum had collapsed. He ran over these shattered bottles.'

'How did these bottles get here?'

'They are the remains of the petrol bombs that the mob had been catapulting through the windows. My dad didn't seem to notice he was bleeding. He was so upset to see mummy lying on the floor and it was only later that we knew how badly he was cut.'

I looked at the jagged edges of the bottles and the burnt

curtains and then realized that I hadn't seen my little foster son. 'Where's Tanko?'

Lucy tried to reassure me, 'He didn't come home from school today. Maybe when he saw the mob he turned back.'

I had brought Tanko into my home three years before when he had been desperately ill with TB. The people in his village believed that witchcraft had been used on him and they were afraid to have him back. I now felt anxious but tried to reason with myself. He was an intelligent lad and hopefully he would be hiding somewhere. I had always warned him about riots and taught him to retreat if ever he saw a mob.

Lucy raised the candle higher as we entered the bedroom and through the dimness I could see the safe. Even in daylight, the mechanism was so precise, that I usually had difficulty in manipulating the combination. This time my hands were shaking and I had to concentrate very hard. To my relief the safe door sprang open. I grabbed the passports, money and keys. There was no time to change out of my filthy clothes; I seized a small case and attempted to stuff it with shirts and trousers. Just as I was leaving the bedroom, I spotted our small laptop and hung it on my shoulder.

Downstairs, Eli had arranged with friends to shelter us until dawn. The commanding officer kept telling us to hurry up. He wanted us to leave through the back entrance. Eli then warned everyone to get away as soon as the curfew lifted. Assured that police would protect the people left in our house we sadly said good-bye. We walked outside through the verandah and into the next compound that housed our bungalows where Gideon's car was parked ready for our escape. Ogbaje and a handful of our most loyal staff followed us as we picked our way into the next garden.

I peered at the outlines of our bungalows. Something was unfathomable. What was different about their shapes? The first one was still smoking. My eyes were searching for the front door and windows when I realized that the roof was missing and some walls were burnt to the ground. I could see the skeleton of our Suzuki Jeep that had been used to fuel the destruction. This bungalow had been let to a voluntary organisation called Abantu. Where were they now? Frantically I enquired after the project staff. 'Where are Omolara and Comfort?'

Ada answered, 'Thank God they went to Enugu yesterday to attend a conference. Some of the mob demanded that we handed Omolara over to them, they knew her by name and they were after her. That was at the start of it all. I even telephoned the Abantu headquarters in London because I knew that we were in serious trouble. All that time we could hear the youths outside shouting at us to bring out Omolara Shola. I surmised that the mob had learned her name from the community radio program on women's rights she had established, with the help of my daughter. Ada continued her story. 'We were very afraid Ma, and so Rebecca ran out to lock the gate but as she was fixing the padlock, a long sword was swung under the gate and someone tried to slash her feet! Luckily she saw it and jumped for her life.'

Rebecca stood there nodding her head and chanting a catechism of praise. 'We thank God for our deliverance. The Abantu people were saved. God in his wisdom took them away to that meeting in Enugu; we thank you Jesus.' She was a pigmy-sized woman, loyal and honest and I was very fond of her. I knew that her prayers and faith would shield her mind from the devil itself. Although she couldn't read well, she always wore a pair of gold-rimmed spectacles to church. I'd occasionally caught a glimpse of her leaving the compound on Sunday mornings, head-tie pushed well forward and wrapper hoisted high around her waist. In her hand was her Bible and she would glance surreptitiously to see if anyone was watching her raising her specs to see where she was going. On the Sabbath she felt at least six feet tall.

The other bungalow where Rebecca kept house had fared somewhat better. The Unicef desks destined for an Arabic school had been used to ignite part of this building that housed my office. Rebecca handed me the front door keys, and despite pleas from everyone to hurry, I felt compelled to go inside. The atmosphere in the burnt room was stifling and I could smell something like newly baked bread. The dozens of bags of flour, stacked ready for distribution to hungry village children were destroyed and all that remained was a pile of soot. In my office nothing had been disturbed. A set of calipers made for a little girl who had post polio paralysis lay on my desk. I glanced around. Valuable documents, records of research, were still neatly filed. This place had been the temple of my work, so vital to my life.

We locked up and moved towards the waiting Peugeot. Shaking hands with our staff, one by one, and hugging Ogbaje, our dear loyal friend, who for years had been as close as family, we slid into the backseat. Bravely they waved us off.

We were dropped at a friend's house, a couple of miles down the road in a quiet residential area. Gideon and the armed police drove away, wishing us good luck. It was now three in the morning.

Stewart welcomed us into their house. His warm Scottish lilt was comforting and I began to feel a tiny breath of hope. He hugged us both and his genuine sympathy and kindness overwhelmed us. Eli was very emotional and we could see that his nerves had been badly damaged and his heart, usually so full of love, had been wrenched apart. Stewart tried to comfort him. 'Relax. You're safe. A secretary from the British High Commission telephoned several times this afternoon. Your son Joe from England heard that you were in terrible danger. He was worried silly. He even contacted the British High Commission seeking protection for you. I gather that he gave them all a pretty hard time.' Eli smiled knowingly. We were only too familiar with Joe's determination and knew that he'd never give up.

At that moment the phone rang and we were pleased to hear his voice: 'Mum? Dad? I've been absolutely frantic. What a relief to hear your voices. When the manager of Abantu phoned me yesterday, from their headquarters in London, saying our house was under attack I nearly went crazy. I've been on the phone all day trying to find out what was happening. The news I heard was so grim. I was afraid that you were dead. Are you safe?'

'Yes, we're safe and unhurt but poor Dad has been through absolute hell. It's such a terrible shock.'

'How soon can you come to England? We've heard the news on the BBC. It sounds terrible over there.'

'We're coming as soon as it's safe to leave.' I had tried to reassure him, but as I replaced the receiver I wondered if we'd ever make it out of Kaduna.

Then Stewart's wife Prue came downstairs clad in her dressing gown. She had been soothing baby Jane back to sleep and gave us both a hug. Always a quiet, practical woman, she was warm and comforting.

'You must be hungry, what would you like to eat?' The thought of eating repulsed us, so Prue made a pot of tea. We talked for a while, mainly about Eli's narrow escape and the ghastly bloodshed that apparently had happened all over Kaduna.

Stewart asked us, 'What are your plans for the morning, how can I help you?'

Unhesitatingly Eli replied, 'We need transport to Abuja at first light.'

'We'll see what can be arranged once the curfew is lifted. You'll definitely be safer there.' We were exhausted and needed some rest, so our hosts showed us to our bedroom where we both collapsed on the bed.

I looked up at the ceiling, my head reeling. A sudden consciousness that Eli must be feeling more dreadful disturbed my thoughts. He normally suffered from hypertension, so how was he coping? The utter despair portrayed on his face alarmed me. I tried to smooth his furrowed forehead. Asking questions would only remind him of the horror he had endured. We tried to relax but the slightest sound would startle us. There was a sudden scratching noise outside the window and I lay there straining my ears. It was a human sound. Looking out through the twilight I was relieved to see a guard, scraping his cooking pot. A sudden high-pitched wailing pierced the night's silence - it came from a nearby Mosque and was a call for prayers. A few dogs started howling a descant with the muezzin as if their spirits were communicating with some mystic force. It was a great relief when we heard Stewart moving in the next room. We jumped up, ready to leave and met him going downstairs.

He looked tired but bore a determined expression. 'The curfew will soon end so I'm going to send a messenger to see if the road is clear. It would be wise for us to get away before any more trouble starts up again.'

We followed him to the front door and saw a man sitting astride a motorbike. I looked at the man's cap and slippers and became greatly alarmed. I feared he would ride to the village and alert the mob. 'Can you rely on him Stewart?'

'He's trustworthy and has been with us for a long time.'

'Stewart, is your driver here?' I was wondering who would take us to Abuja.

'No, he lives in town but I'm driving you to Abuja.'

His words came as a shock. His proposal was quite unacceptable to us and Eli protested. 'You can't do that Stewart. We're not going to drag you into our trouble. What about Prue and baby Jane, they'd be left here alone, you must stay with them, anything could happen today. You could all be targeted for sheltering us last night. The journey to Abuja is so risky.'

Stewart's reply was adamant. 'We've already decided about this. Prue and Jane are going to move to a friend's house away from danger and a driver is already on his way to collect them, he'll be here in a few minutes.' Prue was slowly guiding us towards the carport assuring us that she and Jane would be quite safe.

We had known this brave couple for only a few months. We'd met occasionally at parties and we liked them, but we weren't close friends. Prue had always brought baby Jane to our clinic for her routine jabs. I wondered why they were risking their lives to save us. At that moment the motorbike returned, throttling in through the gate and the messenger wasted no time.

'It is safe to go. The road is completely deserted but you'll have to hurry.' There was no more time to argue. Stewart ushered us into his Mercedes. The messenger jumped in beside him and we both clambered into the back.

We were driven away from Kaduna, away from our home, the home where our children had grown up and the place where we had lived and worked for almost four decades.

Stewart drove us away from the deserted residential area and towards Constitution Road where an army lorry with soldiers was patrolling. I saw some youths hurling stones at the Methodist church; they were armed with cudgels and machetes. The soldiers fired shots and they bolted. Stewart soon caught up with the lorry and trailed behind it, for protection. Along the road, most of the houses were burnt out and I noticed the remains of a car showroom. I had known the owner who was a rich Moslem and I remembered the dozens of gleaming new Mercedes that normally stood on the forecourt. I'd always looked with envy as we passed on our daily journey to the Jacaranda. Now only a charred mess remained; millions of naira had been wasted. I concluded that the Christians didn't turn the other cheek this time. I remembered previous riots when the Christians had been completely unprepared and hundreds of churches had been obliterated.

Stewart remarked, 'We're lucky to be shielded by this lorry. Let's hope they're going our way towards the Abuja Road.'

He had no sooner spoken than we reached the Ahmadu Bello Stadium roundabout. Our route went left but to my dismay the lorry turned right heading into town where a street battle was waging in the distance. The crackle of guns rang out but the bangs faded as we drove over the bridge crossing the River Kaduna. I had expected trouble on the bridge but, apart from rubble, probably the remains of earlier violence, the road was clear. At the next roundabout a large Mercedes joined the road in front of us. I could see a woman and several small children sitting in the back. Her face was partially covered by a veil so I assumed that they were Moslem. Another car was also following us. Then there was a lot of shouting ahead and I realised that we were heading towards a huge mob. 'Are they Christians or Moslems?' I asked the security man who replied, 'I'm not sure.'

Then I asked cautiously, 'What's your religion?'

'I can be either, whichever is needed. If questioned I can answer to the Bible or the Koran.' His reply was reassuring. I looked at his face, covered with the scars of smallpox. Stewart had told me that he was a retired soldier and had dealt with many riots.

Suddenly the Mercedes in front swerved madly from a hail of stones pelted at its roof and windscreen. It was turning back, but too late. Wild looking men hacked at their bonnet, smashed the windows and then started rocking the vehicle, like a boat in turbulent seas. I pitied the distressed occupants and whispered, 'Poor souls, they must be terrified. Let's reverse and run for it.'

The security guard replied, 'Just keep calm. There is no turning back. That was their mistake and see what has happened to them.'

We passed the Mercedes and I caught a glimpse of a terrified woman, trying to shield her children from the onslaught. There was no time to help or to protest because our car was already in the thick of it, surrounded by the mob whose leader looked rough. He leered at Stewart through the open window. 'Where are you going?'

Stewart tried to smile, 'My wife and I are journeying to Abuja to catch the plane to London. We are going on leave.'

I was absolutely flabbergasted by his calm reply - they'd never believe him - I was old enough to be his mother. I didn't think we looked a very convincing pair - Stewart, shorter than me, barely reached my shoulders. Eli kept quiet, maintaining his composure, sitting calmly beside me.

The leader brandished his cudgel menacingly and the youths glared at us through the windows. Their eyes were red and some had daubed stripes of black grease across their faces. 'Are any of you Hausa? We are killing Hausas.'

The realisation that these rioters were Christians came as a relief, but I wondered if they were rational. They were letting out horrendous sounds and looked deranged.

One of the youths then pointed a rusty-looking handgun towards Eli and demanded, 'Where are you from? What's your hometown?'

'Bida - my father was a vicar there.' Eli's voice remained calm.

The leader roughly bashed the bonnet with his cudgel, 'Go.'

As Stewart drove on, I glanced back at the Mercedes, but it had already been torched. Ahead was a T-junction and I knew the Abuja road was not far away but we ran into an even larger mob. Their bawling shouts terrified me and there were dozens of wrecked, burnt out cars. I felt like a hunted beast. We were surrounded and Stewart had to stop.

A machete thumped on the car roof as their gang leader approached, his face gruesomely daubed with red palm oil and white paint. He peered through the window and stared straight at me, his eyes shining like the eyes of a wild cat. His face changed and he was no longer a wild beast, but a person I seemed to know. 'Mummy, mummy, are you travelling?'

Was this a dream? There was something familiar about his features and I tried to picture his face without the war paint. Then the light dawned. I'd seen him at our village health clinic a week before when his infant son had been suffering from severe malaria and had been treated successfully. He showered us with greetings, leapt up onto our bonnet, and sitting cross-legged, gesticulated to the mob to clear the way. Once through, we stopped and he jumped down, waving madly and bowing. 'Good-bye mummy, you'll be alright now. There are no more roadblocks. Safe journey!'

As we headed for Abuja, I sank back in my seat, exhausted. 'Thank God it's over,' I squeezed Eli's big hand and waited for his response.

'It's not over yet. I'll be happier when we reach Abuja.' From the slip road, I could see the expressway ahead. We stopped to pay at the tollgates and noticed hundreds of lorries parked along the side of the dual carriageway. Bewildered drivers beckoned for us to stop, so Stewart opened the car window a few inches. One man came over to us.

'What is happening inside Kaduna? They tell us it's unsafe to go there. Is this true?'

Eli warned him, 'Yes it's true. Don't go there. The people are killing one another and the town has gone completely mad.'

We sped on through desolate countryside, sun-scorched and dried by the Harmattan wind. There had been no rain for months and the parched ground was like a dead planet. Smoky hamlets nestled undisturbed. Occasionally men rode along the laterite verge, their bicycles loaded with baskets of tomatoes, peppers and chickens. They were heading for a local market.

A few Gbagi women plodded along the roadside, heavy sticks of firewood stacked upright in a calabash heaved onto deformed shoulders. The Gbagis believe that their head is the temple of their soul and should be treated respectfully so humping loads on the head like other African women is taboo. Mainly subsistence farmers, their way of life has remained unchanged for generations. When I first went to Nigeria they were called Gwaris but now that is considered to be a derogatory term because it implies backwardness and stupidity. Scorned by the Hausas, the Gbagis toil on their farms growing yams, rice, maize and guinea-corn. With soaring inflation they are often forced to sell their land in order to survive.

At last we reached the giant Zuma rock overlooking the Abuja turn-off. Over the years erosion on the vertical sides has exfoliated hollows that have created a face-like image over the granite surface. The lop-sided mouth changes with the varying lights. There is a lot of superstition connected with this image.

We entered the concrete jungle of Abuja, the new capital, where massive houses and skyscrapers have spread like lava. A magnificent mosque dominates the city; its marble walls, golden minarets and roof gleam expensively in the sun. Nearby, the lavish Sheraton and Hilton Hotels tower. The Abuja skyline is interrupted by a mountain called Aso rock, beneath which lies the State House, its extensive wings surrounded by barbed wire and chunks of anti-tank concrete.

Stewart drove to the British High Commission where we were received with kindness and sympathy. We knew the High Commissioner and his wife well and they invited us to rest in their tastefully furnished house. They booked us on a flight leaving Abuja that night and arranged for Eli to be issued with a British residence permit. Detached from my surroundings, I bathed and waited for nightfall whilst Eli spoke to some of the senior staff, answering their questions and relating his terrifying experience.

After dark we were driven to the airport. There was the usual demand for bribes but we moved through customs, immigration counters and the X-ray screens without incident. Eventually we heard a thundering sound as the British Airways jumbo touched down and roared close to our terminal building. My sense of relief was growing when Eli jumped and seemed startled.

'Look.' I peered into his blazer pocket and saw his cupped hand holding a cartridge. My heart seemed to turn over.

'How on earth did you get that?' Shocked I wondered why the Xray machine had failed to expose it.

'That's the one I kept for myself. When all rescue attempts had failed, our friend Usman warned me to keep this last bullet to use on myself.' I recoiled.

'Give it to me. I'll get rid of it. You can't take it on the plane.' I removed the cartridge from his pocket and walked into the ladies room, hoping to find a waste bin. The newly built loo gleamed, all white tiles, but there wasn't a bin. I returned to the lounge searching for a potted plant or a large ashtray. None … the lounge was now milling with people, mainly expatriates, eager to board. Mission unaccomplished I returned to my seat.

'Did you get rid of it?'

'No. I couldn't. There wasn't a bin. The room was stark.'

'Give it to me, I'll deal with it.' I handed him the cartridge and he walked swiftly into the gents'. Soon he returned, beaming.

'Did you get rid of it? Where did you put it?'

'Like you said, the place was stark and I couldn't hide it.
'So what did you do with it?'

'I left it on the washbasin for everyone to see. I stood it upright like a candlestick.' Aghast by his words, I wondered if he had gone mad. I watched several men entering the gents but they each came out smiling. Then a serious looking man soberly dressed took his turn. I stared at the door, waiting for him to emerge.

'I don't like the look of him. He's bound to report it - he looks the type to make a fuss.' Sure enough the man shot out of the gents and strode swiftly from the departure lounge. Within seconds he returned followed by several officials, including the British Airways manager. They entered the gents and I held my breath. What were we to do? Should we own up? Would the flight be delayed or even cancelled? My mouth went dry. One by one the officials emerged looking puzzled. Last to reappear was the British Airways manager, a broad smile on his face and his hand planted firmly inside his jacket-pocket. At that moment the loudspeaker blared that it was time for us to board.

Stepping onto the ramp I realised that we had lost everything we possessed and that I would probably never return to Nigeria but instead of feeling sad, a strong rush of freedom comforted me and I reminded myself how lucky we were to have survived.

Our plane took off into the night. Below I watched as the sparkling lights of Abuja slipped away and then I noticed some tiny flickering lights, a few remote villages. They were the Africa I loved.

Every event, every situation in which you may find yourself has a positive value, even the dramas, even the tragedies, even the thunderbolt from a calm sky.

Arnaud Desjardins

LONDON
October 1954

It was October 1954 and I had been awarded a scholarship to university. It was my first day. Undaunted by gloomy Queen Mary College, situated in East London's smoggy Mile End Road, nothing could dampen my spirits. At seventeen, my head was full of ideals and ambitions. Home had not been particularly happy and now I was free.

After morning lectures, Betty, my classmate, and I headed for the students' refectory commonly called the Bun Hole, to snatch a sandwich before the afternoon session. A scruffy conglomeration of khaki pipes trailed along the roof of the basement corridor and we could hear rumbles of the Central Line underground trains. We followed the plumbing towards the Bun Hole where we grabbed our lunch and looked around for empty seats. Students shouted at each other through a fug of cigarette smoke, but there in a corner were some vacant seats next to two Africans.

Betty nudged me. 'Let's sit with them. Gosh, they're handsome.'

I had never spoken to a coloured man before and was hesitating when I remembered that I was free to do what I liked, after all I was reading Geography. 'Yes let's. It's all geography - geography field work.'

They were tall and dignified. Nat was an engineering student and Eli was studying for his first MB. Unlike other students, they wore immaculate suits, shirts with stiff collars and silk ties. When we joined them, they stood up and politely eased us into our seats. We asked them to tell us about Nigeria. Nat said he was the son of a chief and Eli the son of a clergyman. We were charmed.

We often met our new-found friends as we journeyed on the tube between South Woodford and the Mile End. Betty and I stayed at the women's hostel called Lynden Hall and Nat and Eli lived in Elmhurst, the men's hall, in the same grounds. Eli shared his room with a crazy English student who kept two boas as pets - they were always escaping.

Every weekend, socials were held at Elmhurst - such fun - and as Christmas approached there was carol singing and dancing. We talked about the important social event of the year, the Charter Week Ball, but I never considered going because I didn't have a long dress and in any case was terribly shy with men.

Eli and I were dancing in front of a blazing log fire at one of these hops when he unexpectedly asked, 'Margaret, will you come with me to the Charter Week Ball?' At that exact moment he trod on my toe and squeezed me. 'Alright?'

I thought he meant was my toe alright and so I replied, 'Yes.'

Suddenly he was whirling me round like a spinning top. He spun over to Nat, who was preoccupied with Betty, and announced, 'We're going to the Charter Week Ball. Are you two coming?' His face was a picture of happiness and I realised how much I wanted to be with him.

The next morning I phoned my elder sister Christine, a final year student reading Chemistry at Northern Polytechnic, and I asked her to lend me her black velvet evening dress.

'Yes, sure you can borrow it. It hasn't taken you long to make friends there - who are you going with?'

I hesitated. 'I've met a fantastic medical student. He's handsome and adorable and guess what? He's coloured.' I heard a gasp and then she was laughing.

'Does Mum know? My God, you'd better not tell her.

Do you remember the scene when I took Ali the Turk home for Christmas? Coloured? Where's he from?'

I took a deep breath 'Nigeria.'

'Wow! - that's even worse. He must be black.' Still chuckling she hung up. Later I collected the dress, expensive, sophisticated but a bit too old for me.

We went to the ball and danced to the Nat Temple band until almost daybreak. On a terrace overlooking the Thames I was given my first real kiss. We floated home; there were no tubes and we couldn't afford a taxi so we walked the silent streets for several miles before hopping onto a trolley bus going towards Whitechapel.

I returned home for my holidays that Christmas, wildly in love with Eli, and could hardly contain myself so I told my mother about the ball.

'Are you trying to kill me?' she shouted. 'Don't you remember, our lowest paid maids were black.' I studied her disgusted expression and recollected seeing pictures of our black nanny Antonia holding my sister, just a tiny baby. That was in Brazil, back in the thirties when my father represented a British steel company over there. My sister and I had both been born in Brazil but my family returned to Britain before World War Two started.

My mother must have spoken to my Uncle Wilfred, my father's brother; we'd been forced to move in with him in 1944 when my father disappeared in Brazil, never to be seen by us again. My mother had been left without a home at the end of the war … a difficult time. Unlike my father this uncle was a niggly little man. Our loathing for each other was mutual. We were having some soup for supper when he struck.

'I saw a disgusting sight when I was on the tube at

Paddington this evening.' His pig like eyes flickered as he continued. 'I saw a white woman leaning on a nigger.'

Shocked, I threw my spoon down and left the table. The next morning I packed my belongings and left. After that episode I rarely went home but took holiday jobs in Dr Barnardo's head office or occasionally worked in a factory. As a schoolgirl I had seen pictures of Seretse Khama's adorable coffee-coloured children. He was the Chief of Bechuanaland who had defied the colonial government by marrying Ruth, a British girl. More recently I had read about Peggy Cripps, the daughter of the Chancellor of the Exchequer, who married a Ghanian called Appiah. I decided to follow my ideals.

Eli passed his first MB and moved to the London Hospital, just a mile down the road from Queen Mary College. My contemporaries went home during the vacations so I was there in London with Eli. We met most evenings and walked in the parks, shared chocolate gateau in Fortes and ate chop suey. We also studied together.

One Sunday morning at Lynden Hall, I glanced out of the window and was surprised to see a familiar-looking black Humber Hawk drive up to the door. I wondered if someone had died in the family so was relieved to see both my mother and uncle. A few weeks earlier my mother had written to tell me that she had married Uncle Wilfred; he was now my stepfather. They both looked stern and ordered me to come home, giving no explanation. Perplexed I followed them to the car. Uncle Wilfred, a tiny man, could hardly see over the steering wheel as he drove towards Slough. He was a lousy driver.

We travelled in silence. Once home my mother led me to her bedroom and handed me a letter. The letter was from Dr

Grove, the warden of Lynden Hall a rather straight-laced woman, who was also a senior lecturer in chemistry.

Dear Mrs Nunn,

I feel it is my responsibility to inform you that your daughter is going about with a foreign student. Not only is he Nigerian, he is coloured.

A huge drama followed. I was appalled that Dr Grove had not first discussed the matter with me. I tried to reason with my mother about Eli, but she refused to listen. She implored me to end our relationship, promising that she'd pay for me to study medicine anywhere, she knew that was the career I longed for - she even offered to buy me a Vespa Scooter. I caught the train back to London, feeling hurt because, at that stage, my relationship with Eli was 'innocent'. My mother also wrote to the Dean of the London Hospital who pulled Eli aside one morning with an amused twinkle in his eye. 'I've received a letter from a very irate woman who says you are seducing her daughter.' Luckily the dean ignored the letter. He patted Eli's back reassuringly.

Eli and I tried to separate several times, but we couldn't stay apart for long and our reunions were heavenly. We both realised that this emotional stress was interfering with our studies, so we decided to get engaged. I rang my mother and told her that I wanted to bring Eli to meet the rest of my family. Eli's father happened to be in Britain at that time, studying at Ridley Hall, Cambridge, so he came along too. We warned him that there would probably be trouble.

I was surprised that my stepfather stayed upstairs. My Aunt Ann and Uncle Tim were in the front room when we arrived. Uncle Tim, who was more interested in horse racing, had been appointed as spokesman. He looked uncomfortable and stared dumbly at Eli's father. Egged on by my mother and Aunty Ann, he asked, 'Where did your people come from? I mean…how were they? Didn't they live in trees and wander about without clothes?'

Eli's father, a great diplomat was aghast. 'Yes, I'm sure you're right,' he shrugged.

Uncle Tim, a simple man, carried on. 'You're worlds apart from us.' Turning to Eli he said, 'Leave our Margaret alone.' He asked me to take off my ring - of course I refused.

Eli's father listened quietly as the arguments became insulting. He had tried to support our engagement but as we travelled back to London I could sense his disapproval. The next day Eli and I decided to separate again but it was not for long.

I took finals and scraped through with a third-class degree, rather a comedown for a scholarship student. I moved on to the Institute of Education in central London; I had decided to be a teacher.

In February 1958 we were married in St Dunstan's Church in Stepney. We had only our grants to pay for the reception, but it was a happy occasion, richer than anything money can buy. As I was led towards the church a flurry of snow fell, the sun shone and everything sparkled as if the earth were smiling. Papa from Nigeria officiated during the service. My family had been invited but not a single member came. I thought of the precious words Eli had once written to me on a postcard: 'If God is for you, who can be against you?' Wonderful friends, students, parents, doctors and missionaries from Nigeria gathered. Even Dr Grove gave us a wedding present, an eggbeater.

We started our married life in a rented room in Hackney. During the fifties and sixties colour discrimination prevailed in Britain. Adverts for accommodation blatantly made it clear, 'no coloureds'. Mrs Jay, our landlady was different.

'I don't mind coloureds … after all we're Jews and we've had our share of persecution. So long as you keep the place clean and the noise down, you can stay.'

Our room was on the third floor of a Victorian terraced house and we shared the kitchen with a cheerful old man. The only loo, usually occupied by other tenants, was on the ground floor. The Jays were furriers and worked like beavers somewhere in Stepney. We kept to the rules and paid our rent, so Mrs Jay was happy. She owned several houses in Hackney and spent Friday mornings, tapestry bag looped over her arm, collecting rents. By evening the all-pervading smell of boiled fish wafted upstairs as she prepared the Sabbath supper.

Rid of outside pressure, Eli and I found peace. Money was often short but we did not starve. I usually shopped in Ridley Road market, jostling and bargaining with the barrow boys. Once a week I collected the head of a conger eel to make pepper soup; it was free and quite tasty served with rice. Was the fishmonger really convinced that I had a cat? Eli bought bananas in Whitechapel market - he knew how to choose the sweetest, those with black spots. In spite of the traffic that made the walls of our house shake and pea-soup fogs, we enjoyed Hackney and valued the friendliness and humour of the cockneys.

It was a relief when Eli passed his second MB, one of the toughest exams to be faced by medical students. He proudly came home with a new stethoscope and could hardly wait to try it on me.

I attended the Institute of Education and found the course easy. For teaching practice, I was assigned to George Green's School in East India Dock Road, rather a tough posting. There was a bus strike at the time so I had to hitch lifts to school on lorries that were heading for the docks. Clambering up into the cabin was not easy because I was heavily pregnant.

On the nineteenth of September our daughter Caroline was born in the London Hospital. Eli was exuberant and rushed out to buy a pink carry-cot and bath. He had almost used up our entire allowance. I was too weak to sit up but we held hands and gazed at our beautiful love baby. In spite of the huge haematoma on her forehead - the result of my long and agonising labour - she was like a doll with masses of wavy black hair, dark eyes and a sun-kissed complexion. The haematoma gradually disappeared as she opened up like a flower.

We were greatly surprised when my mother announced that she would visit; we assumed she wanted to see her granddaughter. Eli was at College when she arrived by taxi. Her behaviour was aloof but she leant over the cot peering at Caroline. Tearfully she said, 'Poor child - a half-caste. You realise she'll never be accepted in this world. What a pity. She'll be the one to suffer - not you. Have you thought about that?' Refusing my offer of tea, she departed looking miserable. She had not held her granddaughter.

Memories of my childhood and cold upbringing surfaced and made me determined that our home would be different. The mingling of our two cultures would enrich our children's lives; it would never be to their disadvantage. They would have the best of both worlds … I would make sure of that. A few days later a Silver Cross pram was delivered to our home. My mother had paid for it. Later that week, a large food parcel arrived from Fortnum and Masons. We wasted no time in frying the tinned ham, the delicious smell making our mouths water. Eli and I swallowed our pride and feasted.

When Caroline was six weeks old I returned to teaching. Depositing her in a day nursery was a painful wrench but we could no longer survive on Eli's grant. My first day at school was the worst; my breasts dripped with milk. I wept silently in the staff kitchen.

I had chosen Clapton Park because it was the nearest secondary school to Caroline's nursery. Listed as a comprehensive school, it was an amalgamation of three run-down secondary modern schools. The classes were large and ill equipped. There were hundreds of pupils - many passed through the school hardly known, and disgruntled teachers seemed to be strangers to each other.

I was the form-mistress of the eighth stream of third form and immediately understood that several of the girls in my class worked on the streets at night. They boasted openly about their sexual experiences; their territory was around St Pancras.

Miss Simmons, the biology teacher, befriended me. Together we were assigned to teaching sex education - rather daunting in view of the girls' varied backgrounds. The L.C.C. education department provided a film. As expected, the film showed tadpoles and chickens and progressed to mammals and eventually to humans. As we were arranging the classroom, a memo came from the headmistress, stating that inspectors would be coming to observe our class.

Miss Simmons was apprehensive. 'Make sure you waste plenty of time before starting up the film,' she instructed me, 'pretend the projector is faulty, anything to reduce that dreadful question time that comes after the film has finished. Remember, keep the lights off when the film ends because I'm bound to blush.' Poor Miss Simmons was a spinster who had devoted her life to teaching. Near to retirement she found it increasingly difficult to cope with those girls.

In spite of my fumbling delay tactics the film finished before the bell, so there were a few minutes left for questions.

Agnes Talbot raised her hand, cruelly eying Miss Simmons. 'Miss, when's the safe time?' There were some giggles followed by a ghastly silence. My colleague was speechless and I suspected she didn't understand the question because she looked blank and then embarrassed.

I decided to help her. Placing my hands on my pregnant tummy, I smiled. 'There is no safe time.' The inspectors beamed and the class cheered.

A week later I was offered 'head of geography' with a special responsibility allowance of £220. I did not accept because I knew I would soon be leaving.

Loathing having to leave Caroline in a day nursery and longing for Eli to qualify, I stuck it out. We moved into a larger flat with a bathroom and kitchen - sheer luxury after Mrs Jay's single room.

Eli qualified on the seventh of December 1960. It was the same day that our son was born. It was also the time of the Notting Hill riots; on my way to the London Hospital, heavily in labour, a rough looking man had brandished a crow bar at us. Whitechapel was blanketed in snow and the trolley buses were unable to run. Andrew was a thin baby with straight black hair and his fine features made him look more Asiatic than African. Throughout my pregnancy I had avoided eating too much fearing that I might face another difficult birth. When I looked at Andrew I was filled with guilt.

Once discharged from Mary Northcliffe Ward, I was deposited at our flat; Eli feeling reluctant, had to return to the London Hospital to take up the post of resident house surgeon. Alone in that dismal flat with two babies, I felt depressed. The following six months dragged painfully because Eli had no official time off. Occasionally I would lug Caroline and Andrew to the London Hospital hoping to meet Eli for a few hours, but invariably he was called to casualty. Disappointed, I would trundle home boarding the last trolley bus and struggling with my two sleeping babies. Members of the Salvation Army would look at me quizzically. They probably thought me irresponsible keeping young babies out late at night.

Eli chose to serve his second house job at the Royal Victoria Hospital in Dover because it offered married quarters. We moved to our new seaside home aware that in about six months we would leave for Nigeria.

My mother and uncle had moved to Ramsgate. My mother had not been well and the doctor had suggested that her illness was psychological. He had advised her to make peace with us. She telephoned, inviting us to lunch.

Caroline, aged two, delighted my mother by dusting the furniture and chatting like a canary. My uncle held Andrew, gazing into his eyes and crowing as he rocked him. Andrew had grown into a handsome child and resembled my real father. I had never before seen my uncle show any affection. As the afternoon passed, we all became gentle with each other, believing we would never meet again.

My uncle seemed particularly sad and said, 'Never let these children forget me'.

I was perplexed by his display of emotion. I never saw him again. He died of lung cancer soon after we settled in Nigeria.

Moving to the Royal Victoria Hospital in Dover was heavenly, a real change from the smog of London. Caroline, rid of her constant chest infections, had become a little girl. She had always been prone to convulsions and I hoped that all that was ended. Andrew, a good-natured baby, crawled around the communal doctor's lounge, contentedly chewing anything he could grab - he seemed to have a preference for lumps of coal.

I would load both children into the Silver Cross and stroll for hours along the seafront; during the summer months I played with the children on the pebbly beach. Eli, under constant pressure as a house surgeon, spent endless nights on duty. He barely had time for breakfast and would rush away to the operating theatre to assist his temperamental surgeon.

Hospital food was ghastly and our quarters had no kitchen. I was allowed to use a small fridge for Andy's baby foods but as it was also used for bottles of blood, I managed without.

Eli passed his driving test and bought an old banger costing seventy pounds. Immensely proud, we named it Archie but unfortunately the gears were unpredictable and it became my task to support the gear stick especially when Eli drove uphill. The steepest gradient was at St Margaret's Bay - a great challenge. During one expedition the long stick shot out of my hand on the steepest bend. Archie started to roll backwards and cars tailing us had to rapidly reverse. We could not stop laughing as Eli battled with the gears trying to make a hasty getaway.

We would have preferred to stay in Dover for an extra six months so that Eli could gain experience in obstetrics and gynaecology, but orders from Nigeria Office were clear – he had to return home. We therefore packed, sold Archie and used the proceeds to buy a small Hoover washing machine.

We left Dover in the early morning hoping to spend a couple of hours in London before catching the boat train to Liverpool. We went to Swan and Edgar's in Regent Street.

'You'll need some cotton dresses for the voyage,' insisted Eli, 'Lagos will be steaming hot.'

I knew that we had less than a hundred pounds and resisted but Eli was already choosing two.

'Go on, try these and stop wasting time.'

Reluctantly I slipped on the first dress, pink with rose bud borders. There was a cardigan to match. I tried the second dress, pale turquoise voile, so feminine. The dresses were wrapped and I felt like a queen.

We next visited their photo studio where several months before - still living in Hackney - we had taken Caroline for her photograph. Some friends had later mentioned that they had seen a large portrait of our baby in the window of Swan and Edgar's.

Eli asked for the manager. 'There was a photo of our daughter on display in your shop window some time ago and we would like to buy it.'

The manager looked puzzled but seemed to remember us, he went to search in a cabinet. Soon he returned with the poster-sized portrait. Eli and I looked at each other. We knew that we had to have it.

'How much is it?' I asked.

He shrugged 'It's not for sale.'

I could hardly believe his words but Eli was undaunted. 'What good is it to you? You've made use of it, now you should allow us to buy it.'

The man thought for a moment. 'Twenty-pounds. I'll let you have it for twenty.'

Eli nudged my arm as he firmly queried, 'Who gave you permission to display our daughter's portrait in your window?'

'No-one.'

'Then this could be a matter for my solicitor.'

The man twitched nervously. By now Andrew was bawling loudly and other customers were growing impatient.

'I'll let you take it for a fiver.'

Eli pretended to look annoyed and extracted three pounds from his pocket. One by one he placed the notes on the counter. 'This is what I will pay you. The photo is badly faded. You should have asked for my permission before exhibiting our baby in your window.'

The man hastily wrapped the picture in cardboard and tissue paper. Victorious we left the store, hugging the portrait and laughing as we rushed to catch the boat train to Liverpool.

It was evening when we boarded the Aureole. We were shown to our cabin towards the back of the ship and after a light meal crashed onto our bunks. We were too tired to stay up and wait for the ship to sail and, in any case, would not have seen much, because it was foggy. I hugged Eli, excited that by morning we would be in the Bay of Biscay.

I was wakened the next morning by a strange noise. The children were still asleep and it came from Eli who dashed out to the loo, retching. I was perplexed because our ship was rocking so gently ... surely he couldn't be seasick? I remembered those nauseous weeks of my early pregnancies when Eli had suggested that my sickness was 'purely psychological.' He returned looking ill.

I pushed open the porthole, hoping to feel a rush of sea air. 'Fresh air is the best thing. You'll soon feel better. It's just psychological.'

But where was the sea? I could only see grey - a grey concrete wall - we were still tied up in the docks, fog-bound.

We disembarked at Freetown on New Years Day 1962 and there I stood for the first time on African soil.

On 4 January 1962, we sailed into the Lagos Lagoon, the cabin doors were flung open and many flamboyantly dressed Nigerians emerged. They had hardly ventured from their cabins throughout the entire voyage. Sailing along the Lagoon I admired some beautiful houses and tall buildings. I spotted a Union Jack floating in the breeze and noticed a splendid house with terraced lawns leading to the water's edge. It was the British High Commission. Nigeria had gained independence in October 1960 and at that time had been described as a jewel in the sun and the great hope of Africa.

We disembarked at the Apapa Docks to pandemonium. The noise was unbelievable; manners were thrown into the lagoon as people pushed and jostled, shouting and arguing with customs officials. Heavy trolleys of luggage were hurled in our direction. Dazed by the shouting of Yoruba people - their way of greeting - I thought they were fighting. I grabbed the children and held them tightly whilst Eli battled to retrieve our luggage. Soaked in sweat and stifled, I started to feel panicky. Completely hemmed in I could hardly endure this unimaginable heat. I looked for other Europeans, wondering how they were able to cope, but discovered I was the only white person there. In spite of the crowds, Eli's relative, Amos, managed to find us. He was an evangelist, and had travelled from his village in the north. He was unaccustomed to Lagos.

Eventually the Crown Agents helped Eli to find our loads. We were then taken to the Ikoyi Rest House, several miles away. There the agent handed Eli our rail tickets and departed. We would travel north by train the next evening.

Our bedroom was a chalet with two shallow sided cots and a bed with no springs. All were draped with dusty mosquito netting. Andrew and Caroline were grubby and needed baths so I attempted to run some water. A trickle of rusty sludge dripped from the tap and that was all. I put sleeping Andrew in his cot and went to search for a steward. To my dismay, Andrew must have woken; he fell over the shallow side of his cot and landed with a terrible thud on the concrete floor. A huge lump came up on his head. I tried not to panic but throughout that night I sat beside him, listening to his breathing and fretting over my crude introduction to Nigeria.

The next evening we boarded the train bound for Kaduna. Our compartment was small and the loo stank. Some of Eli's cousins came to see us off and handed us a tray laden with fish pepper stew, fried plantains and rice. These people were not wealthy but had brought out their most precious bone china; I felt humbled by their kindness.

Our journey north would be over six hundred miles. The train jolted and halted throughout the night, never seeming to exceed twenty miles an hour. We ate the fish stew ravenously but the red pepper stung my mouth. I needed to drink but the water was not safe. The only drink available was Star Beer, brewed in Kaduna - a strong lager in large bottles. Eli laughed when I downed one large bottle. Unaccustomed to beer, or any alcohol, I slept like a log.

We are the sum of a huge number of free actions for which we are the only ones responsible.

Matthieu Ricard and Trinh Thuan

THE NORTH
January 1962

In the early morning I awoke shivering with cold. The savannah vegetation showed through the mist. Eli explained that we were in the northern region and the cold harmattan wind was blowing from the desert. After about eighteen hours our train crawled into Kaduna. Eli's sister, Margaret, met us together with her husband, James, and their two infant boys. We stood in the shade of some gigantic mahogany trees and waited for our luggage. Above, perched on the branches were scores of vultures. For the next few days we stayed with the family in a large colonial style house situated in Churchill Avenue. Margaret could not have been kinder and she obviously adored Eli. She guessed that I would find Nigerian food strange and offered me her stove to cook English food. She cooked with firewood and the heat in that kitchen was overpowering. I struggled to cope with the Nigerian diet but palm oil was used in the daily stew and I found it nauseating. The boiled rice smelt of dirty socks and the sight of green slimy okra repulsed me. I tried to keep smiling but sometimes it was impossible.

Eli's parents lived in Bida, a town situated a hundred and fifty miles from Kaduna. I wanted to meet them. I was growing anxious to know if they would accept me.

A friend offered us all a lift in his Opel car and picked us up one morning at daybreak. We sped through the silent streets of Kaduna and were soon on the main trunk road linking Lagos with the Northern Region; as this was a strategic road I was astounded when a few miles outside Kaduna the tarmac ended. The road surface changed abruptly to laterite, red and was corrugated by heavy tankers and trailers that perpetually plied this route.

To rid ourselves of the choking dust we wound up the

car windows but soon the heat inside the car became stifling. Already my throat was red raw - apparently this was a common ailment during the harmattan season. Our car rattled over the uneven surface jarring our spines, especially when the sump struck hard rock; at times I thought the chassis would split. Caroline and Andrew fell into a deep sleep; their bodies had shut down from the vibrations.

I clenched my teeth in apprehension when we crossed narrow unguarded plank bridges that traversed deep gullies. We were forced to give way to oncoming lorries that bore down on us at high speed, bullying and never slowing ... or were their brakes faulty? They forced us off the road into thick sand. It was not surprising that there were so many wrecked vehicles straddled along the verge; twisted metal and tangled bodywork, often crushed beyond recognition.

A red film of dust masked the scrub-like bushes and the monotony of this arid landscape was only relieved by termite hills that towered like fairy tale castles. A herd of antelope leaped across our path and families of baboons, hugging startled young, would stare at us defiantly through the bushes. After several uncomfortable hours we reached Tegina where shacks lined the roadside. Numerous motor mechanics waved spanners and fan belts at us, hoping for repair jobs, especially punctures. Our driver spoke bitterly of previous encounters when tintacks had been deliberately scattered along the road surface. The only filling station appeared to be derelict but jerry cans of fuel were sold everywhere. After Tegina we turned left and the landscape became greener. Fan palms rose out of swamps and we gradually descended into a valley.

One lorry had nose-dived into a grassy patch... its rear end protruded and boldly displayed a brightly painted picture of Jesus with the words 'And He leadeth me into green pastures.' We were frequently stuck behind overloaded lorries that swayed dangerously and belched black smoke. To overtake blindly would be to dance with the devil.

Before entering Zungeru, the old capital of the Northern Region, we had to drive over a long railway bridge that spanned a river gorge. Trains, vehicles, cattle, donkeys and pedestrians shared this narrow bridge. As a train was due the road before us was closed. We were hemmed in by herds of long horned cattle that pranced about, horns clashing as the bulls fought for dominance; fearless children tapped on our windows selling hard-boiled eggs, grubby looking bread, peeled oranges, cough sweets and bottles of river water. One trader invited us to buy a dead creature that looked like a crucified rat - definitely a rodent, splayed out on crossed sticks. Eli explained that it was a bush rat or Grass-cutter. Amused at my horrified expression he informed me that it was considered a delicacy. Women sold smoked catfish that smelt like kippers, flies swarmed everywhere. Eli said that dried fish was added to stew to make it tastier. I wondered how our children would survive the diet in Bida.

Eventually the train appeared and rattled slowly across the bridge; passengers were crammed inside the carriages and some were hanging on to the outside and straddling the roof. At last the barrier was lifted and our driver carefully steered the wheels of the car onto the shining railway lines … surprisingly our wheel span fitted perfectly. Through the steel girders I could see the river gorge deep below where fishermen tossed circular nets into the swirling water and canoes, laden with passengers, were paddled through the strong current. Beautifully-shaped mud houses with steep thatched roofs lined the grassy banks. I was acutely aware of the challenge that lay ahead. Gazing across the savannah I felt that I could sense the very soul of Africa … there was no going back.

Once away from the hubbub, we paused for a break beside a steep hill. Relieved to stretch, we clambered up the rocks searching for shade. We could see the silver river meandering in the distance. We had reached Nupe country and Eli breathed in deeply and stretched his arms towards the sky as if to embrace his homeland. He was home at last after years of studying in England. He closed his eyes and whispered to me, 'I am back with my people and can feel the spirits of my ancestors.'

We ate our picnic of fried rice and hunks of fried goat meat … I would have dearly loved a cheese sandwich, and longed for a slice of bread. Eli sat with Andrew in his arms and talked about his boyhood. 'I used to travel to school by canoe. There were three of us who went from Bida to Holy Trinity School at Lokoja. We saw crocodiles and hippos in those days.'

How different our lives had been. I was aghast that a child could be sent away by canoe to a school so far from his village.

'Wasn't it dangerous … you still can't swim?'

Eli swatted a tsetse fly off Andrew's head. 'Of course it was very risky but I was lucky to gain admission to the Holy Trinity School. Those were hard times. Papa was determined I would have an education. I lodged with a family called the Sangoes and served as their house-boy, chopping firewood and sweeping their compound - the hardest job was carrying kerosene tins of water from the River Niger. I carried it on my head for a distance of over three miles.'

'It's amazing that you survived all that.'

Eli looked serious. 'I nearly didn't. One day I was playing on a canoe and slipped over the side into the river. The current swept me away and I thought I was drowning. Like a miracle I drifted back towards the bank. My school friends were screaming and shouting and by the time I reappeared James was actually praying. He's now a bishop.'

Shocked by Eli's story I asked, 'Did you tell anyone what happened?'

'Goodness no - I would have been given a severe beating. After that I became very ill. I must have swallowed pints of river water. One of my teachers noticed how thin I looked and he sent for my mother. It was lucky for me that he cared because I had caught amoebic dysentery.'

Grabbing Caroline who was busy chasing a lizard I felt conscious of the miracle of Eli's very existence and longed to hear more. 'Did you return to school after you got better?'

'Oh yes. I studied like mad and came top and in 1947 won a scholarship to Wusasa Middle School. From there I went to the C.M.S. Grammar School in Lagos.'

I pictured the struggle Eli had endured in order to be educated. In the entire north of Nigeria he was the fourth indigene to qualify as a doctor - the first Nupe doctor. I admired his determination and glowed with pride.

As we continued our journey, I noticed how friendly the Nupe people were. They waved and greeted us as we passed through numerous villages.

The sky changed from gold to pink and the huge sun was sinking behind some sandstone plateaus when we drove into the Mama compound.

A driveway shaded by Melina trees led to the Church Mission Society compound where Papa lived with the Mama family. On the left were two school buildings, with black shuttered windows and dilapidated thatched roofs. To the right I noticed a small church, built of mud: beyond that was a brick house where two English missionaries lived. The house facing us was the family home. Its walls had once been whitewashed.

I heard shouts of excitement as a crowd of people rushed towards us; the women were ululating to express their joy. As we clambered out of the car a forest of arms seized Caroline and Andrew, hugging and squeezing them as they were passed from person to person; our children were too astonished to protest.

I could hear a repetitive chorus of, 'Ku be boe, ku be boe, ku be boe,' meaning, 'Greeting in your tiredness.'

Eli and I responded, 'Ku be mi, Ku be mi, Ku be mi,' meaning, 'Greetings with your home.' This strange chorus continued for several minutes, reminding me of a gaggle of geese roused by an intruder. Occasionally this chorus would diminish only to start all over again, more loudly. After several minutes the words shortened to, 'oku,oku, oku,' a soothing monotone.

The women wore woven wrappers, loose blouses and colourful head-ties. Many carried babies on their backs. Children were everywhere, pushing their way to the front where they stared, round-eyed, touching and smelling. The crowd respectfully parted as Papa wearing his cassock came to shake our hands - I sensed his genuine warmth. Eli's mother followed closely, her hands outstretched as she led the welcoming chorus. She was a stately woman … tribal marks were engraved on her high cheek-bones and bluish tattoos covered her dark cheeks. Her narrow eyes, partly closed after years of exposure to the glaring sun, seemed more Chinese than African.

They led us into a small sitting room where the shutters were already closed against mosquitoes and flying insects. Oil lamps were being lit. The family gathered and I was introduced to Eli's sisters and only brother as they approached in age order. Janet was the eldest followed by Lucy, Winifred, Victoria, Dorothy and the youngest and the only brother, Theophilus. Margaret had remained in Kaduna. I sensed they were scrutinising me closely as they giggled and whispered to each other in Nupe. Some more adventurous children stroked my hair; I guessed the slippery texture was strange to them.

Lucy, tall and slim, was a schoolteacher, married with three children. She resembled Mamma, especially around the eyes. Janet, a nurse, had a rounded figure and a smiling, welcoming face despite widowhood … her husband had recently died of liver cancer. She had four children, the youngest less than a year old. Victoria, training to become a nurse, was small in stature and more reserved. Eli had spoken proudly about his youngest sister Dorothy, who was clever and had won a scholarship to a reputable Secondary School.

It seemed that the family parlour was brimming with welcoming people and I began to realise the magnitude of the Mama family - how would I ever remember all their names? One older woman with a wooden leg was eager to greet me. She was called Mama Pataco, translated from Nupe it meant Mama Peg-leg … Eli whispered that she had once lived with an English man. Aunty Alice Angulu was a handsome woman and particularly warm to me. She was Mamma's half-sister; her husband, a sincere man, was also a vicar. At that time he was translating the Bible into the Nupe language. The Angulus were struggling to educate their children - their handsome sons, Michael and Uriah, were on vacation from university.

Conversation was mainly in Nupe - I could hardly understand a word. Through the dimness I looked around, adjusting to my new family. Every few minutes one would look at me reassuringly murmuring, 'Oku, oku.' I responded, conscious that I sounded like a contented crow.

I crept away to the backyard to search for Caroline and Andrew. A fire glowed and two women squatted over it, stirring a pot of palm oil stew. Others fried plantains, gently turning the diagonally cut pieces in the bubbling oil - the smell was better than Yorkshire pudding and made me feel hungry. Women were pounding steaming hot yam in a wooden mortar - the rhythmic beating of the long pestle sounded like drumbeats. An elderly woman was busily chopping leaves and adding them to a liquid that bubbled over the fire. I realised that a feast was being prepared.

Caroline and Andrew raced towards me wearing just pants … they had discarded their clothing, including new Start-Rite sandals and were a picture of grubby happiness. Hand in hand with their cousins they were chasing a bleating goat.

We were eventually summoned in for supper and our plates were laden with delicious looking food. We waited while Papa said grace, thanking God profoundly for our safe return, blessing my mother and stepfather back in England and remembering those recently departed.

At last we were able to eat. I plunged my fork into the yam and dipped it into the red stew. Holy smoke! Was I eating fire? Chilli pepper burnt my mouth painfully. I pushed the gravy to one side and quickly chewed a mouthful of plain yam but it was too late. My mouth and oesophagus stung terribly and my eyes and nose watered. I beckoned to Eli urging him to stop our children, and I filled my mouth with earthy water, swilling it around before swallowing.

After the meal small children cleared the dishes and a bell clanged for prayers. Everyone knelt on the hard floor with hands together and eyes screwed tightly shut. Papa prayed devoutly first in English and later in Nupe. I could hear mosquitoes pinging in my ears and occasionally biting. Gradually other members of the family added to the prayers. One youth seemed highly excited as his raised voice implored Jesus. I wondered what he was asking for - it seemed a sizable list. I peeped at him and noticed his face puckered with frowns. I wondered if the good Lord ever grew tired. Caroline and Andrew were already sleeping on a chair.

We were eventually escorted to our sleeping quarters behind the church. Following a beam of torchlight along a grassy path, Eli staggered with Caroline in his arms and warned me, 'Watch where you tread, there may be snakes.'

The round house where we were to sleep was clean and whitewashed. It was the mission guesthouse. Some very solid wooden beds had been made up and I noticed that the bed-sheets were brand-new. Buckets of well-water had been provided for washing. Through the candlelight I peered up at the steep thatched roof. The high- pitched chirping of crickets was deafening. Holding a dim torch I visited the outside loo that consisted of a small drum surrounded by grass matting. Alamanda bushes hung overhead. As I was peeing I heard a rustling sound in the overhanging twigs - I fled. That night we tucked the mosquito netting tightly under the mattresses - fearing that a snake could slither through the open shutters. Two weeks later I was about to hop into bed when I noticed a brownish heap between our sheets. A young python was in residence.

After spending two weeks in Bida it was time for us to

return to Kaduna. We boarded a train from Zungeru. I felt utterly drained. I thought back over our stay in Bida. What a failure. But there had been good moments so I tried to focus on the happy times.

We had visited the Emir in his palace, a memorable experience. His bodyguards, dressed in bright green and red, like the Pied Piper, had drummed and chanted praises as we entered a magnificent palace. The thick walls and flat roof were made of mud, intricately designed. Colourful enamel bowls studded the walls as decoration. We had been made to remove our shoes before entering his throne-room. Beneath a large turban sat a giant of a man. Eunuchs fanned him with ostrich feathers. The Emir ruled the Nupe people, though he was actually of Fulani origin. He was a descendant of fierce conquerors that had ravaged the North of Nigeria and introduced Islam.

The other highlight of our visit was when Papa took us along the river in a canoe duck shooting. He was an expert hunter. He showed Eli how to take aim, but it was difficult to balance without capsizing the shallow canoe. As we paddled along the riverbanks Eli pointed to some large water birds. 'We were never short of meat when we were children. Papa was an expert hunter. We used to trek for hours, searching for bush-meat - we hunted by night.'

Papa was smiling as Eli continued, 'We were so poor - in those days it was most unusual for all eight children to survive. Mamma did well.'

I loved animals and detested the idea of destroying wildlife but I could appreciate that hunting for food had been a necessity. I was curious to hear more. 'Papa, what did you kill, was it just birds?'

Papa was delighted to recount his hunting adventures and beamed. 'I shot anything we could eat. Usually it was guinea-fowl and partridges but once I shot a bush cow.' His expression changed as he became serious. 'It nearly had me because it sneaked up from behind. Its angry snorting warned me just in time. As it charged I shot it through the heart.'

'What else did you kill?'

I detected a mischievous glimmer in Papa's eyes. 'Snakes, bush pigs, antelopes and monkeys.' Noticing my shocked expression he added, 'Monkeys are tasty, especially served with plenty of red pepper.' I hoped he was teasing me.

The family stew never appealed to me. Chicken heads, beaks and feet were all tossed into the pot. No part of the animal was wasted. I realised that Eli's sisters avoided serving these unusual parts to me. Eli had spoken to Lucy about my food - 'Margaret can't take pepper - it makes her ill. Why do you continue to use it?'

Lucy had looked very hurt. 'My brother, we aren't adding any chilli to Margaret's food. You must understand that Mamma's groundnut oil is already peppery from the grindstones.'

How I wished that I felt stronger. I had wanted to join in with the cooking and pounding of yams but my body was weak from the intense heat. Eli's family had made a tremendous effort to keep us happy ... I hadn't done very well.

Lucy had taken me aside one morning trying to familiarise me with Nigerian customs.

'When you marry a Nigerian, you marry the whole family.' I was pleased to hear this but she added, 'If you were an African wife, Mamma would bring up your first-born child. Apart from feeding you wouldn't be allowed to handle your baby.'

I felt threatened. Nobody would take my child away.

Perhaps the main reason for my unhappiness that day, as we travelled on the train to Kaduna, was that Eli and I had just had our first big row. Mamma had offered us a young houseboy who was slightly retarded. I envisaged he would be more of a hindrance that a help. To make matters worse his head was full of powdery ringworm. I did not want him and was adamant. Eli lost his temper.

'Leave these matters to me. Don't interfere. Mamma knows what is good for us.'

This young gormless looking youth sat there in our carriage. His hair had been shaved and his ringworm was now painted with gentian violet. He looked at me with sad brown eyes. I realised that I pitied him. I would give him a chance but his ringworm still worried me.

Whilst Eli was visiting the hospital and the Ministry of Health, trying to sort out his appointment, we stayed with Eli's sister, Margaret, and her family. I soon became ill, with a high temperature and aches and pains like flu. Worst of all was the headache. I shivered all morning and waited for Eli to return. He felt my head and took me to the laboratory for a blood test. The slide showed malarial parasites.

The doctor on duty seemed puzzled when he saw the result with three plusses.

'Which prophylactic are you taking?' Eli, inexperienced in tropical medicine showed him the remains of the Daraprim tablets we had been given in Dover.

The doctor scowled when he saw the packet. 'Daraprim is no longer effective in Nigeria - these days we are having breakthroughs with patients on Daraprim.' He cracked a glass vial open and drew some liquid into the syringe. 'This type of malaria in Nigeria is one of the most virulent strains in the world. You don't play with it. You must change to chloroquine phosphate.'

The injection stung my arm but I was too weak to care. After that I went to bed with blurry vision and slept heavily.

The next day Caroline crawled into my bed. I felt her body, and she was burning with fever. Her face was twitching. Eli and I rushed her to the Nursing Home where Dr Audu, the specialist paediatrician, was called. By mid-day she started having convulsions. Her temperature remained high and, despite numerous injections and tepid sponging her convulsions would not stop. We both knew that Dr Audu was a brilliant doctor, but he was not God. By late afternoon Caroline fell into a deep comatose sleep. We sat beside her bed terrified that she would die. That evening Dr Audu examined her still body - his expression was grave. 'I'm afraid you may lose her. The likelihood is that the temperature will rise - it always does in the night. She can't take much more and there is very little else I can do. She has cerebral malaria and even if she survives it's likely she'll be brain-damaged.'

Eli and I were devastated. My panic gradually changed to grief. I gazed at our beautiful child lying there like an angel. We had nicknamed her 'Poupee' because she was our little doll. She had been so happy in Bida and so full of life … I prayed silently, pleading with God and promising that I would help other children in need.

I had already learnt that life was precarious in Nigeria. Everywhere children were dying from hunger and neglect. Now I knew what it would mean to lose a child. This must have been the worst moment in my life.

An English nursing sister came on duty that evening.

Extremely capable and sympathetic, she stayed with us throughout the night, tenderly nursing our daughter.

The next morning Caroline woke up, bewildered by her new surroundings. We tried to keep her calm to prevent more convulsions ... gradually she recovered.

After that ordeal, relief followed, but I had lost my grip and broke down completely. 'Eli, take us back to Britain. I can't stand much more. This is no place for our children.'

Eli held me tightly in his arms and whispered, 'Yes, darling. Don't cry. We'll go just as soon as it can be arranged.'

I believed he meant it but still wanted to be certain. 'Do you promise?'

'Yes, I promise.'

The next morning a taxi drew up at Margaret's house. We were surprised to see Lucy who we had left in Bida climbing out with her three children. She was carrying Funmilayo, her five-year old daughter and struggling with Tunje, her toddler boy. Her eldest son Victor was trying to drag a heavy holdall from the boot.

Eli, delighted to see Lucy, rushed to help, 'Ku be boe, Ku be boe,' but his greeting stopped short when he saw the expression on Lucy's face. 'What's wrong? What has happened my sister?'

Lucy's voice was quieter than usual. 'After you left Bida, Funmi started with this high fever. I thought it was malaria and gave her chloroquine tablets but the fever wouldn't go away - it grew worse. See how she's struggling to breathe. She keeps crying about pain in her legs.'

Lucy gently rested Funmi on the couch, stroking her forehead, whilst Eli put his stethoscope to her chest. He pressed the muscles in her legs and gently flexed her knee joints, his face became grave. 'She'll have to be admitted to hospital. I don't think this is malaria. It's the pain in her legs concerns me but I can't be sure. Has she been immunised against polio?

Later that night Eli returned distraught. 'I'm sorry to say that Funmi has polio.'

Funmi survived but the polio left her crippled.

***

The Northern government eventually provided us with housing, a spacious bungalow in a quiet road close to the hospital. Our sitting room had large windows that provided cool cross ventilation, and attractive terrazzo floors shone like polished granite. The smell of newly dried paint and putty lingered for ages as a reminder that we were the first occupants. There were two wings, separated by a courtyard, one for sleeping and the other for living. Eli and I were overjoyed with our new home. We started digging and planting - apart from a single mango tree the land was bare.

When Eli's first pay cheque came, ninety pounds, we were in a dilemma. Our massive windows needed curtains for shade and privacy but we could not resist buying a small radio instead. We were feeling cut off from the outside world and could hardly wait to tune in to the chimes of Big-Ben.

Eli's salary would barely support us so I applied to the Ministry of Education for a teaching job. There were no vacancies in secondary schools but after several weeks I was offered work at the Capital School, a primary school, mainly for the sons and daughters of top government officials. I dropped Caroline and Andrew at May Beamish's nursery and hurried to my first day at school.

Roger Baker, the headmaster, was standing under the front porch, his generous stomach hung over his baggy drill shorts. After his good-natured welcome, he led me along the veranda to class three. Children's chattering hushed when we entered the classroom. Roger pointed out different children and boomed forth. 'That boy is the son of the Minister of Education. This pretty girl's the daughter of the Minister of Finance. That small boy over there, his father's the Commissioner of Police.' I looked around the room more fascinated by the children than about their father's positions. There were many different nationalities - Indians, Syrians, Lebanese, British and Nigerians. I knew I would enjoy teaching them.

Later I learned how Roger Baker struggled to maintain high standards and how his appointment was constantly threatened if he disagreed with eminent parents. I could see that these children were very fond of him - he maintained good discipline and was always fair. The children in my class were mainly eight year-olds. As the weeks passed, I began to understand their backgrounds. Most of the Nigerians were Moslem. Their fathers lived in large government quarters where branching passageways led to extensive wives' quarters - such families had many children.

One day a limousine drove into the school compound and two men clad in brightly coloured robes climbed out. The clerk seemed to know them and led them straight into my classroom. They strode past my desk, ignoring me. Their eyes darted from child to child until they recognised a small girl - a bright little pupil. Grabbing her elbow, they led her outside to the curtained limousine. I followed but my protests were ignored. The clerk kept reassuring me, 'Ba kome, Ba kome.' (It's nothing.)

The older boys were sniggering when I returned to the classroom but one girl raised her hand. 'Today is her wedding day - she is going to be married to the Emir of Bauchi.'

I challenged the sniggerers. 'What's so funny about that?'

An older boy, still amused acted as the spokesman, 'The Emir of Bauchi is an old man. He is very fat.'

'Ba kome, ba kome - it's nothing.' The clerk's words raced through my mind; I was filled with fury that gradually melted into sadness and concern for that eight-year-old girl. To such men it was nothing - nothing like that would matter - she was merely a female.

After school I collected Caroline and Andrew from nursery and later picked Eli up from hospital. Waiting there in the hospital compound, parked under a mango tree, there was a terrible stench coming from the mortuary. Dilapidated buildings housed dismal wards, rubber sheets and soiled linens were draped over railings and beggars wandered everywhere, pushing enamel bowls at me. 'Give me dash, dash me Madame.'(money). I looked at their palms - some had fingers missing due to leprosy.

Eli came to the car one afternoon looking particularly dejected: 'I've had an awful day. I had to give medical examinations at the prison. Some prisoners needed to be certified fit for execution. I thought I was meant to save lives, not destroy them.'

No wonder he looked downcast with such an appalling responsibility. 'Didn't you fail them?'

'No, that's the worst part. They had the healthiest bodies I've ever seen. I even suggested symptoms, but they refused to let me help. It seemed as if they wanted to face their

75

punishment. I will never visit that prison again.'

As weeks went by it became clear that Eli loathed working in the General Hospital - he spoke emotionally about the conditions. 'The place is filthy. There are cockroaches in the incubators and dirt everywhere. The syringes are stained and the needles are used over and over again until they're blunt. If I make the correct diagnosis what's the good? There are not enough drugs. I'm wasting my time.'

During the night, Eli would be called to the maternity ward where girls, as young as twelve, who had struggled for hours to deliver their babies at home were brought in, often too late. Some bled to death because their uteruses had ruptured; their bodies had not finished growing. Some young girls were torn so badly that they had vesico-vaginal-fistulas, a chronic condition that leaves them with an offensive odour. Such women are doomed to be social outcasts, nearly always spurned by their husbands.

At least two hundred people queued in outpatients every day. Eli was the only doctor on duty, by afternoon he came home drained. 'The worst part is that many are malingering, they waste my time and delay treatment for those who are genuinely ill.'

His unhappy expression concerned me. 'How do you know who's faking?'

Eli's frown cleared, 'I look at their tongues. Horace Evans, my old teacher at the London Hospital, taught me to always examine the tongue - that's what I do. A healthy pink tongue means you're fit, but a coated pale tongue, a cracked tongue, or a bright red tongue is always a warning sign.'

On 30 October 1962, Eli resigned from the government and started his own practice in the heart of

Kaduna. His resignation shocked government officials. The Minister and the Permanent Secretary spoke to him harshly and warned him that the Sardauna was displeased. Ahmadu Bello was the Sardauna of Sokoto, and a very powerful leader of the Northern Region. He summoned Eli to his office and vented his fury but this verbal battering left Eli undeterred.

After Eli's resignation we had to quit our government accommodation and pay back our car loan. My monthly salary of a hundred and twenty pounds helped us through those turbulent days. Eli rented a small building from the 'Assemblies of God Mission,' an American evangelical church, and there he opened the Lafiya Clinic. In Nupe language the word Lafiya means health and peace. This was the first indigenous private practice in the Northern Region. It became Eli's Utopia, a clinic where he maintained the highest standards in medicine. Before long patients crowded into his small waiting room. Many were traders from the market and clerks from the local banks; some were not well off but those unable to afford the consultation fee of five shillings were never turned away.

We needed to rent a family house but most landlords demanded at least one year's rent in advance. Eventually we had to manage with a small bungalow in a dense part of Kaduna. The road was dusty and there was litter everywhere. The tin roof, heated by the sun, made our rooms unbearably hot. Opening the small windows only exposed us to greater heat and dust.

Our neighbours were mainly Hausa people and before long Caroline and Andrew made friends with their children and learnt to speak the language fluently. We soon grew accustomed to the call for prayers from a nearby Mosque and enjoyed seeing the children colourfully dressed celebrating Sallah, a religious festival.

One day we were invited to a naming ceremony. Long before daybreak we could hear the sound of drumming and praying. The baby boy to be named was just a few days old. During the ceremony a barber cut tribal marks on his tiny face using a cut-throat razor. He also shaved the baby's head - as his scalp was pulled taut, the fine cuts opened and bled. A dark looking concoction, a mixture of herbs, was pressed onto his fontanel. This part of the ceremony is supposed to give protection from evil but it worried me for I realised he was too young to have been immunised against tetanus.

Kaduna developed rapidly in the sixties. New factories sprang up including the second largest textile mill in the world. Eli was appointed company doctor to several firms and before long we were able to rent a larger house in a pleasant residential area in South Kaduna. In the cool afternoons Eli and I played tennis at the Kaduna Club and Caroline and Andrew romped in the playground with their school-friends. Tall buildings were constructed along main roads and the mighty Hamdala Hotel was opened. We swam in the Olympic-sized pool. Our lives were crammed with work, sport and parties, mostly with expatriate friends.

Many British wives had very little to occupy their days. They employed cooks, stewards and gardeners; very few were granted permits to work. Their children were usually sent to boarding schools in Britain - there was no better option. Coffee and bridge occupied their mornings followed by sports, especially golf and tennis, horse riding and polo. At weekends there were curry lunches and late night parties; for a few, heavy drinking and wife swapping was the main occupation. Eli and I made life-long friends during those golden years. Very few Nigerians held parties because they were mostly Moslem: they were forbidden to drink alcohol and their wives were usually kept in purdah.

On 10 June 1964 our son Joe was born - how different from having a baby in Britain. Janet, the capable nursing sister who had helped to save Caroline's life, delivered him in our home - she later became his godmother. To celebrate Joe's rapid emergence into the world the three of us sat on the bed and toasted our new arrival with shots of Courvoisier. I gazed at Joe, our third child. He was perfect - I was too excited to sleep. I had given up teaching and would enjoy this baby.

Eli applied for a loan to build our family house and it was granted. We spent hours with the architect debating over the design. We chose a reputable Italian construction company to build. One morning we were visiting the site when Eli's brother-in-law drove up in his Triumph car. He looked agitated. 'You'd better go home quickly, there's going to be trouble.'

Eli looked alarmed. 'What's happened?'

Dennis took Eli's arm and led him to a corner, away from the workmen. 'The Premier has been assassinated.'

Eli clutched his brother-in-law's arm. 'That's impossible.'

'It's true. I went with the television crew and I saw his blood splattered on the bedroom walls. He had been shot several times.'

Dennis was a senior civil servant and worked in television and education. I knew he was speaking the truth when he warned us, 'There are bound to be recriminations. Kaduna could become a bloodbath - you had better go home and stay indoors.'

A picture of Ahmadu Bello, the Premier, flashed

through my mind. He was massive in appearance, his height accentuated by his huge turban. He was frighteningly powerful and had always seemed indestructible. He had thousands of followers in the North. He was also a spiritual leader directly descended from Usman Dan Fodio, the Fulani warrior who had conquered the north in ancient times and introduced Islam. The full implication of the Sardauna's assassination dawned on us. It was 15 January 1966. We went home and stayed there for the rest of that day.

Later we learnt that Abubakar Tafawa Balewa, the Prime Minister, had also been murdered. A modest, thoughtful leader, he was also a northerner. Igbo army officers had staged that first coup. These assassinations ended the prosperous golden years for Nigeria. We were aware of the ferocity of angry Moslems: 'An eye for an eye and a tooth for a tooth' is their belief. We expected immediate reprisals but Kaduna remained stunned and quiet, abnormally quiet.

Eli and I longed to move to our new house. We were still living in Kaduna South on the far side of the river. I realised that I would miss Maureen, my wonderful neighbour. She was a Chinese Malaysian, also married to a Nigerian. She cooked tasty Chinese food and kept her house immaculate. Her first baby was just a few weeks younger than Joe. We were like sisters, sharing jokes and commiserating over problems as we pushed our babies in their prams on long walks together. Maureen worked in the military hospital as an almoner, she knew many army officers.

Another friend was Rita Miles; her husband was the general manager of Kaduna Textiles. One morning in September 1966 Rita and I went to swim in the Army Pool close by the river. Caroline, Andrew and Joe were splashing in the water and we could hear the voices of kingfishers in the overhanging trees.

We were unpacking our picnic hamper when Rita's husband appeared. Fred, a calm, reserved man, seemed ruffled.

Rita teased him: 'Darling, don't tell me you've come to swim?'

Fred, normally submissive, especially with Rita, was not amused. 'It's terrible. The Moslems are slaughtering Igbos near the market. It's very bloody and is likely to spread. I've come to take you home.'

We packed up and left. Fred drove Rita in his car and I loaded my tiny Fiat and followed. As we drove across the bridge to Kaduna South, I saw mobs by the roadside. They had tied Igbos to vehicles with long ropes and were dragging them at high speed.

My limbs were trembling when I reached home; I hoped our children were too young to understand what they had seen. Much to my relief Eli came home early from tennis. We sat down to supper but could hardly eat. We heard screaming and shouting coming from neighbouring houses. The next day we learnt that most of the cooks and stewards along our road had been beheaded.

Around midnight some men came to our front door - they rattled the glass and shouted impatiently. Papa had given us an old shotgun and I went to the bedroom for it. Eli opened the door and I crouched on the stairs, hidden behind a solid banister, and pointed the barrel at the intruders. If they laid a hand on Eli, I would shoot them. I strained to hear what was going on and picked out some words in pigeon English … I realised they were Igbo. They needed help with a badly injured man.

The next morning a young boy called James came to our back door looking terrified. He normally lived with his uncle, who was a corporal in the police, and often played with our children. I wondered what had happened. 'Come in James. Are you alright?'

Tears welled up in his eyes. 'My uncle packed his bag and went away last night - he hasn't come back.'

My cook and gardener, both northerners, were in the kitchen. 'Ma, he's an Igbo - best you send him away. The Hausas are still searching for Igbos. If they find him they will kill him. It's dangerous to shelter an Igbo.'

I could see that Thomas and Buba were worried. I reasoned with them: 'His uncle has disappeared. How can I possibly send him away? He's just a child.' I cut a hunk of bread and handed it to James who ate it ravenously. He was a polite boy, always ready to help. His features were not particularly Igbo, except for his bushy hair. There was no time to waste. 'Thomas, fetch scissors and a razor from the bathroom.' Thomas soon returned with the razor. 'Now help me to shave his head. We'll make him look like a northerner.' Thomas worked like a master barber but James' newly-shaved head looked lighter than his face, so Thomas found him a Hausa cap. I knew our plan would work and I trusted my allies. Days later when the violence abated we were able to send James to safety in Lagos with money stitched into his northern attire.

Rita phoned me later that morning. She was always immaculately dressed and made up, not a hair out of place. One always thought of her as being totally self-obsessed, but her next words showed her concern for the country and its people. 'Would you come and help me at the railway station? Hundreds of Igbos are trying to leave. They're in a terrible state. I hesitated, considering my position as an English woman married to a northerner … a tricky situation because it would seem I was siding with those who had killed the Sardauna. 'I'd like to come, but I'll have to speak to Eli first.'

'When you come, bring all your empty bottles and some powdered milk, and bring any food and clothing you can spare.'

I replaced the receiver and turned to Eli. He looked thoughtful and gave me a squeeze. 'Of course you can go but for God's sake take care.'

Rita was waiting. Her bungalow was close to the railway station so we walked across the main road carrying boxes of beer bottles filled with milk. Outside the station were Hausa mobs trying to get onto the platform. The police were holding them back but they allowed us to pass through the barrier.

There was a train drawn up on the platform, its carriages crowded with Igbo men, women and children crying and groaning in distress. Many were bleeding from machete wounds and I noticed some men with their tongues cut out and others dying with their throats slit open. Rita, normally dainty and vivacious, turned pale. I was shocked and did not know how to face such horror. I spotted some Irish priests I knew because I had played golf with them; they were struggling to distribute food and clothing. Before I had time to retreat one spotted me.

'There's a woman having a baby. She's been like that for hours. Would you help?' Rita and I followed him to the crowded carriage. The young girl in labour looked weak and it was clear that she needed a doctor, but to take her back through that mob would be fatal.

'When's the train leaving? How much time have we got?'

The priest shook his head in exasperation. 'Nobody knows.'

Somehow I managed to reach St Gerard's Hospital and return to the station with a doctor, in an ambulance. We were able to drive right onto the platform. The nun gynaecologist confirmed that the patient required surgical intervention. The mob obviously did not know what was happening as they just stared at us and allowed us to pass. Our patient was lifted onto a stretcher and together with her husband we sped away. Rita was left with a difficult task because the worried father-to-be had shown reluctance to leave his two bicycles. Rita managed to drag them to her house ... difficult because they were chained together. I said she deserved a medal.

Later we learnt that the train was ambushed at Kafanchan where the passengers were massacred. The birth of that baby boy had saved his parents' lives. Years later, the father returned to collect his bicycles and thank us.

In the days that followed, riots spiralled out of control as mobs murdered tens of thousands of Igbos who lived in the north. One northern commanding officer called Hassan Katsina said: 'Coups succeed coups - there will never be peace again.' Unfortunately his predictions were correct ... he later became a general and a military governor. Ojukwu, the Military Governor of the Eastern Region, an ex-Etonian, warned all Igbos to return to the east, and thousands streamed home. Ojukwu, unable to accept the federal authorities, declared the oil rich east an independent republic and named it Biafra. On 6 July 1967 a Civil War broke out. It was during this war that my mother visited us in Kaduna in December 1967.

My stepfather had been dead for five years and my mother had mellowed with age. Eli and I discussed our feelings about her past behaviour and concluded that she had known no better and had acted within the limits of her understanding. There were other mixed marriages but ours was one of the few successful ones. These were transitional times in more ways than one. We moved to our new house the day before my mother arrived. I was determined to show her every aspect of my life in Kaduna. Our house-staff, having great respect for age, courteously came to greet her. After they had left, I witnessed her puritanical, Victorian perspective.

'Poor things - obviously they are being forced into all this disgusting sex. Just look at all those children. They must be breeding like rabbits. How can they possibly feed and educate them decently?' The situation was compounded when I took her shopping in the main market where she saw flies swarming over the meat. From that day, she refused all balanced meals and insisted on a diet of imported cheese and biscuits. She watched trader women passing our house carrying loads on their heads and babies on their backs. 'It's a disgrace - they're working like beasts.' Over dinner, she recounted the day when, as a child, she saw a black man walking along the street in Stanley, Yorkshire. It seemed he was later one of the exhibits at a fair where the locals paid pennies to see him. My mother would never change; she saw Nigeria as 'niggeria' and looked at her surroundings through the lens of some bizarre racist who saw all Nigerians as primitive. When she voiced her strong views, I was highly embarrassed.

In spite of her bigoted attitude, she adored our children and they responded. She spent hours helping with their homework, bathing and caring for them. By the time she returned to England they adored her.

The cruelties I had witnessed in Nigeria had left me with a bitter taste. My trust in humans had been shaken and I grew anxious when I considered our children's future. I had always thought that human behaviour was rational but now I had learnt that man is a dangerous animal. Eli and I remembered our pledge ... our children would be given the best of both cultures. I wondered how this would be possible.

At this time I had moved on to teaching in Queen of Apostles College, a Catholic Convent. I had been trained as a secondary school teacher and wanted to move forward in my career. At the best I was a nominal Christian but I was strengthened by this experience. My students, both Moslem and Christian, were keen to learn: the nuns were like angels, always helpful and warm towards me. Caroline was accepted as a pupil in the first form and although very young, she came top in most subjects.

By January 1970 the Biafran war ended but it had claimed tens of thousands of lives, especially in the east. Many of our British friends had left Nigeria after the Igbo massacre, especially those who had witnessed their staff beheaded; others quit as the civil war spread nearer. The Government subdivided Nigeria into twelve states and the nation was once more on the move as families returned to their roots. The Governor of the North Central State that included Kaduna announced the take-over of all private schools. Queen of Apostles unexpectedly became a government school and was re-named Queen Amina College, after a ruthless Queen from ancient history. The gentle nuns witnessed statues of the Madonna pushed aside, as they were forced to leave. There were hardly any graduate teachers left in the north and consequently education suffered. Sister Anne, a young nun, came to see me before she left for Ireland. Sad to see the deterioration of her school, she spoke with emotion. 'Caroline is a very clever child - she is particularly gifted - she needs more challenge. It would be best if you could send her to boarding school.'

Eli and I talked the matter over. There was a civil war going on in the south; it was hardly safe for her to travel in Nigeria. London was just five hours away by plane. We decided to let our ten year old 'little poupee' go.

Leaving Caroline in an English boarding school was a heart-rending ordeal. I could foresee she would find it difficult to adjust to this more restricted life. Our children had enjoyed tremendous freedom in Nigeria. They loved to run along the riverbanks with our dogs, peer into the deep pools of water and clamber up rocks. Caroline, alert to wildlife in the countryside, could recognise different species of birds, butterflies and wild flowers. She lived cocooned in her magical world often expressing her feelings in painting and piano playing. She made friends with our gardener's daughters Laruba and Lami and they played together for hours, swinging, clapping and skipping. She shared her toys and they let her taste their peppery food.

I felt pangs of doubt and regret when I hugged her good-bye, trying to suppress my sadness. She must have sensed my pain. 'It's all right mummy. I'll be brave - I chose this myself, you didn't force me to come here.'

I caught the next plane back to Kano where Eli met me. We both felt sad as we drove back to Kaduna but I was determined to concentrate on Andrew and Joe. They were both keen at sport and regarded schoolwork as an unnecessary chore. Andrew was particularly physical - I began to doubt my ability as a teacher when my attempts to coach him failed. Education in Kaduna had deteriorated and most teachers were indifferent to their work. Eli and I worried about Andrew's future. Should we send him to Britain? Eli disagreed. 'He'll never settle in a British school. Andy's more African in his ways - his future should be here in Nigeria. I want him to grow up as a Nigerian.'

I felt differently. 'He needs motivation. He'll never learn anything here - his teacher doesn't even bother to mark his work.'

Eli adored Andrew - they were similar in many ways. 'Don't you think I want the best? Sending him to Britain is not the solution.'

When Andrew reached eleven he sat the Nigerian common entrance examination. The results were eventually published but his name and number were not on the list. We were advised to visit the principal of Government College who, we were told, would probably be able to locate the missing results.

Our appointment was scheduled for ten in the morning but we were kept waiting in a dusty corridor for over an hour. The principal's door was slightly ajar and we could hear him giving instructions to the school gardener and later talking to some female who was obviously not his wife. With difficulty Eli suppressed his annoyance, conscious that patients would be waiting for him. At last we were permitted to enter.

Behind a bushel of jumbled papers sat the principal. For several moments that seemed like an age, he continued to write. I studied his face, noticing that one eye bulged and moved independently like that of a chameleon. I wondered if his mind was as muddled as his desk? His body language made it clear that he did not care a hoot about Andrew's missing exam result. As we left I heard him mumbling to Eli and I recognised the word 'goro' meaning 'kola-nut'. Surely he was not asking for a bribe?

That was enough. We sent Andrew to boarding school in England and he settled well. There were several other Nigerian boys in his class and they became firm friends. Joe soon grew restless to join Andrew. He was only eight but longed for the fun of boarding school. He was not making much progress at school in Kaduna so we reluctantly let him go. By 1972, our three children had fledged and the house became silent.

The Biafran war had ended in 1970. General Gowon, the new President, had been Eli's junior in the Wusasa Middle School. He and many other senior officers had been trained at Sandhurst. Nigeria had become a corrupt nation and Gowon failed to check the financial excesses of his state governors. He was a popular leader but was considered too lenient. In 1975, when Gowon was abroad, a group of Northerners staged another coup and Murtala Mohammed became the next President.

The new government immediately took control of the civil service and the National Security Organisation or secret service embarked on what was described as a 'purging'. Ten thousand civil servants were relieved of their duties ... some were terminated unfairly after years of service. Yet many Nigerians, sick of seeing the rich flaunting their wealth, admired Murtala Mohammed for fighting corruption and greed. He didn't remain in power for long, and Eli and I were surprisingly close when his assassination took place.

In February 1976 we drove to Lagos to play golf in the

Lagos Open. Eli was a great golfer and played off a handicap of one. We had decided to take a break to celebrate our eighteenth wedding anniversary and booked into the Atlantic block of the Ikoyi Hotel. This luxurious skyscraper building now replaced the old Catering Rest House where we had spent our first night when we sailed in from Liverpool. Lagos was worlds apart from the north - there were fashionable shops and extravagant restaurants. People drove along the pot-holed streets in expensive Mercedes cars. Eli and I yearned for the golden beaches of Lagos - the lush vegetation was pleasing after travelling from the dry north. This was to be our second honeymoon.

After breakfast on 13 February, we loaded our golf clubs into the car ready for a practice round. We drove out of the hotel car park and headed for the Ikoyi Golf Club but there was a go-slow. Vehicles were not moving so after a while we managed to turn back to the hotel. I noticed groups of people clustered together in the car park - some looked agitated. 'Look Eli, something must have happened - people are listening to their car radios.' We switched ours on and heard that President Murtala Mohammed had just been assassinated in an attempted coup. He had been shot as he travelled to work right along that road we had taken to the golf club.

Nigerians flocked to sign books of condolence. I was surprised that Murtala Mohammed, only six months in office, should be mourned so intensely. Was it mass hysteria? Gradually I realised how much the people liked him but I also wondered if some of the victims of his purging would be celebrating. Public protests and student riots followed. At night Eli and I, high in the Atlantic block, peered down onto the streets of Ikoyi. We stared at tanks and lorries loaded with soldiers doing night patrols. We heard occasional gunshots during the night curfews and assumed there was trouble within the army. On 15 February 1976, Eli and I ventured out to some nearby shops. We wanted to buy something special to cheer us up and to celebrate our anniversary. We chose a silver ice bucket with tongs ... a real treasure. We still have it though it is tarnished with age. Later that week we drove back to Kaduna.

Earlier that year Eli had been elected President of the Rotary Club of Kaduna. Our friend, Colonel Bissalla, had invited Eli to use the officers' mess in Kaduna for his special inauguration party. Colonel Bissalla was a well-educated, eloquent man with a gentle loving wife, not a typical soldier. Before Murtala Mohammed's assassination Bissalla had been promoted to the rank of Major General and Minister of Defence. We wondered about his safety.

One evening a few weeks later Eli went to Rotary and I switched on the television. To my horror I saw General Bissalla, bound to a stake about to be executed. I studied his gentle face, half smiling and fearless. Then a black cloth was bound over his eyes; the executioners took their time.

Altogether thirty people were shot after that attempted coup. Utterly sick and alone in the house, I moved into the study and played a Chopin nocturne on the piano. This tune will forever haunt me as a reminder of our gentle friend.

The next morning I went to comfort his wife. At first the soldiers would not permit me to enter her compound but I pleaded in pigeon English. 'Make you allow me de enter. Na you be soldier. What if dis ting go happen to you yourself?' The gates were rapidly swung open. Mrs Bissalla greeted me bravely. She was clutching a flat box.

Lost for words, I hugged her. I knew she would soon be evicted and offered to assist. 'What about packing? Let me help you?'

Mrs Bissalla shook her head. Her grip tightened on the box. 'This is all I need to take.' She was holding some gramophone records of Handel's Messiah.

***

During those years when our children were in boarding school I spent many months in Britain, especially during their half-term holidays. My mother was growing old and less able to drive on motorways but she never missed a chance to visit the children and looked forward to their exeats. The added responsibility gave her a new lease of life and broke the monotony of her lonely existence.

Although Eli and I missed the children during term times, we grabbed any opportunity to travel abroad and have fun. We both worked hard and needed these breaks. On one occasion we decided to attend a Rotary Convention in Brazil. I had always wanted to revisit Rio, the city of my birth. After Brazil we planned to fly on to Washington to meet old friends, before returning to Britain in time for the children's holidays.

It was a stiflingly hot evening when we boarded a British Caledonian Jumbo at Gatwick for our fourteen-hour flight to Rio. Once airborne, drinks were served and, after we had flown over Madrid, trays of dinner were handed to passengers. Feeling relaxed we started to eat. I had squeezed lemon over my smoked salmon and taken my first mouthful when the stewardess unexpectedly removed my tray.

'Hold on,' I protested, 'I've hardly started.' I noticed

her face was unusually flushed.

Before Eli could prevent it, his tray had also been grabbed - the trays of all the passengers were being swept away - then the sound of the engine changed as the plane tilted to one side. Conversations ceased and the cabin gradually became silent.

Eli took my hand and whispered, 'We're turning, there must be something wrong.'

An announcement followed: 'Would you all return to your seats and fasten your safety belts.'

When the stewardess came to check the passengers, Eli asked her, 'What's going on?'

The young lady was unable to conceal her nervousness. 'I'm not allowed to say - but there is a problem.'

Eli asked her to come closer and spoke in a low voice. 'What type of problem? Is it engine trouble?'

She shook her head. 'No, the plane's alright.'

Eli persisted. 'Then what is it? I bet it's a bomb.'

Her hand went to her mouth. 'The captain doesn't want the other passengers to know because it'll cause panic.'

Eli was not going to let her go until he had heard more. 'How do you know there's a bomb?'

'The captain received a radio message from London. The IRA telephoned that a bomb has been planted on a British plane bound for Rio tonight. This is the only flight to Rio out of London.'

A second announcement came: 'Ladies and gentlemen, you will probably have noticed our plane has turned. We are returning to Gatwick. There is a minor problem but no cause for alarm.'

'No cause for alarm?' I faced Eli. 'Are they joking? I'm

alarmed - I'm very alarmed - I'm bloody terrified.' I fell back in my seat although my instinct was to leap onto it and scream, but what good would that do? My arms went limp and I could feel my neck throbbing.

I noticed beads of sweat on Eli's forehead but he managed to force a smile. 'We'll be alright.'

I remembered the life insurance I had taken out only hours before leaving Gatwick. What was the good? We were the only ones in our family to know of its existence. I thought of our boys sleeping peacefully in their school dormitories, and Caroline in University, whilst Eli and I were 'gallivanting to Rio,' as my mother had so aptly put it. I tried to think how to cope with this fear. Gatwick was at least three hours away … then it occurred to me: 'Eli, I don't think we're going to die, but if we are, let's die happy.'

He turned to me and raised his eyebrows quizzically. 'What do you mean?'

'I mean, let's have some champagne.'

'Good idea.' He pressed the button; the pink-faced stewardess appeared.

Eli, managing to retain his poise, smiled at her: 'Would you bring us some champagne … and make sure it's cold.'

An ice-cold bottle of Moet et Chandon was brought to us on a silver tray. We were parched after the heat at Gatwick and drank as if it were lemonade. Soon our giggling was the only sound to be heard in the cabin.

When the plane landed there where dozens of fire engines gleaming under arc lights. We were hustled into a coach whilst the luggage and plane were searched - a lengthy ordeal, and an uncomfortable one due to the diuretic effect of the champagne.

Four hours later as we were allowed to re-board, we noticed security police guarding a single piece of unclaimed luggage - a brown paper parcel. We never discovered if this was the bomb or if everything had been a hoax. Our flight to Rio was exceptionally comfortable because there were many empty seats.

Rio de Janeiro was wonderful. We went to the top of the Sugar Loaf Mountain, swam in the sea at Copacabana and searched for the Strangers Hospital where I was born - unfortunately it had been demolished. There was also a more sinister side to life in Rio. The steep hillsides skirting the city were where the favelas lay. These dilapidated slums housed the poor, strongly contrasting with the rich lifestyle of many wealthy Brazilians who had entertained us so lavishly. Most Brazilians were ashamed of these unsightly slums. They constantly warned visitors of muggings and crimes but it appeared that little was being done to help these desperate people. Eli and I talked about similar slums in Ibadan and Lagos and agreed that they are a disgrace to any nation. My memory of babyhood was rekindled. I could remember very little, except for a feeling of love and warmth towards my nanny.

We enjoyed the Rotary convention and heard Mother Theresa address an audience of over ten thousand Rotarians. She looked tiny and her voice was frail. Her words were brief and difficult to understand, the huge audience applauding loudly. I had read about the wonderful work she was doing in Calcutta and was filled with admiration for her courage. It would be many years before I would appreciate how profoundly her example would influence me.

By the time the holiday ended I began to feel like a cat

with nine lives. During the Rotary Carnival some exuberant Brazilians threw confetti at us. I opened my mouth to laugh and inhaled a large piece that blocked my windpipe - I choked and thought I was going to die.

Later when landing in Washington our plane overshot the runway - the engine let out a roar as the plane climbed steeply, narrowly avoiding buildings. Most passengers were sick. Relieved to be alive and slightly shaken, we disembarked and that was where I caught sight of Concorde, resting there like a white swan ... the temptation was just too much. 'Let's change our tickets back to London ... I want to fly on the Concorde.'

Eli was still feeling shaken. 'Go ahead. Change them if you want to.'

Flying on Concorde was an amazing experience. As we climbed through the atmosphere the plane bumped, reminding me of cycling over cobbles. I began to feel tense and glanced at Eli. 'I don't like this very much. If I had known it would vibrate like this I wouldn't have come.'

Eli, not looking too happy, took my hand. 'You devil. It was your idea - I would have been quite happy to fly home on the Jumbo.'

When the bumping ceased, engine sound became silent as if it had been switched off. We looked down and saw the curvature of the earth, a glistening planet illuminated by the sun. Every indentation along the east coast of America stood out like a huge map. We peered upwards and saw the sky was jet black. Trying to adjust to these strange sensations, I touched the side of the plane and noticed it felt hot, from the outside friction.

After we had feasted and sampled the most exquisite

wine, Concorde passed through the sound barrier: later we travelled at twice the speed of sound. There was something spiritual about that whole trip … it made me view life differently and I began to question my lifestyle.

***

Our children were growing up and gradually they moved on to university. Within the confines of boarding school, they had been sheltered and protected from the outside world - now they were free. Remembering my crazy student days twenty years before, I felt anxious about leaving them alone in Britain. At the same time I was determined not to intrude on their lives knowing that it would only drive us apart. We bought a small holiday home near my mother in Kent; Eli had accepted that I would have to spend more time in Britain.

It was during this time that my mother fell and broke her hip - the start of her deteriorating health. She needed moral support so I stayed with her for several months until she was sufficiently rehabilitated. Within a year, her hip replacement failed and the operation had to be repeated. Once again I returned to Britain and after that visited her every few months. Whenever I had to return to Nigeria, she would be tearful and depressed. 'I won't be here next time you come home,' were usually her parting words. Worry and pangs of guilt cast a shadow over my life.

Meanwhile, during my long absences from Nigeria, Eli continued to work. He did not complain but I knew he must have felt neglected. Being the eldest son he faced heavy responsibilities towards his family; he therefore spent much time in Bida, his hometown. He built his parents a large family house and provided funds to educate the children of numerous relatives. There were many distant relatives in his village in need of support. His mother and sisters, all strong Christians, constantly reminded him of his financial duty towards the church. At times it seemed that their requests were never-ending. I wrestled with my conscience, inwardly annoyed by the pressure imposed on my husband who visibly aged during those years. Papa, the Reverend Solomon Mama, was wise and understanding, always appreciating our help: I respected his advice and felt close to him. I kept reminding myself that I had chosen to marry a Nigerian and, traditionally the eldest son is responsible for his ageing parents and family. I suppressed my anger, realising that bitterness would spoil our marriage.

The rented premises of the Lafiya Clinic were becoming increasingly crowded. Traders set up shacks around the entrance, already congested by buses and taxis. Eli had applied to the government of Kaduna State for suitable land to build his dream private hospital. He had submitted many applications, but The Ministry of Lands and Survey repeatedly lost his applications. Instead of apologising, they bombarded him with more red tape. His was the first private clinic but doctors from other parts of Nigeria were acquiring land easily.

'You're not seeing the right people,' his friends advised him. 'You don't know how to be a Nigerian.'

Eli became increasingly discouraged. 'Why should I lick their boots? I'm not a beggar.' He gradually turned to his roots in Niger State where he was offered a perfect plot of land for a hospital. He planted orchards and sunk boreholes and every weekend would fly in an eight-seater plane to supervise the construction of his ideal hospital. It took several years to complete.

There were shady courtyards, cool clean wards, a fine laboratory and a spacious outpatient waiting room. Eli was determined to provide good, hygienic medical facilities for his people. The cost of building this hospital amounted to millions. Later, it turned out that many patients expected free treatment whilst others were too poor to afford the small consultation fee, less than fifty pence. Eli had made a tremendous effort to build this well equipped hospital but it turned out to be a financial disaster.

As his parents were fast ageing, he felt the need to spend more time in Niger State. The thought of living there filled me with dismay. The climate was unbearably hot and I felt sapped of energy whenever I stayed in Bida.

I tried to come to terms with these problems, sometimes feeling confused and afraid. Moaning to Eli would have thrown us further apart - I had known several mixed marriages fail due to pressures from the extended family. I valued our marriage and knew that Eli was a good man facing the normal responsibilities of an eldest son. The uneducated people from the village found it inconceivable that he could ever be short of money especially since he could afford to have a white wife. I was being tugged in three different directions, between teenage children, Mother and Eli.

When there's a disappointment, I don't know if it's the end of the story. But it may be just the beginning of a great adventure.

Pema Chodron

OUTSIDE KADUNA
1981

During one of my stays in Britain, Eli phoned from Kaduna. I could hear that he was tickled about something.

'Guess what? We're building a pottery.' I could hardly believe his words. We both enjoyed visiting the old Abuja Pottery built by the famous pioneer potter, Michael Cardew. Together we had often wandered in the village markets around Bida, collecting decorated traditional pots. But this latest idea seemed like a wild dream. 'What on earth made you think of doing that? Who'll run it?'

After a hesitation, there was a chuckle, 'You, of course.'

Rather daunted, I protested. 'I know nothing about ceramics. Who is the real person involved?'

'Darling, I thought you'd love having a pottery. It would be such fun. I know how much you like pots.'

It was later that Eli explained how he had been introduced to a talented young potter called Simon who had just qualified in ceramics from the University in Zaria. He wanted to work in a pottery but very few existed in Nigeria at that time; he had approached Eli for a small piece of our farmland where he hoped to build a kiln and workshop. It turned out that he had no money so Eli agreed to sponsor him.

Although my initial reaction had been negative, the thought of building a pottery actually appealed to me. Michael Cardews's old Abuja Pottery lay between Bida and Kaduna. I had often stopped there, mesmerised, seeing those Gbagi potters throwing and coiling superb pots. The materials used in the Abuja Pottery were local: clay was dug from the ground and the rocks for glazes were gathered from various locations in the north. The pots were fired in a wood kiln where the flames licked them, creating an earthy quality. On the surface all seemed easy. Of course I was wrong.

I happened to be in England at a time when many pottery workshops were being established, especially in the west of England, so I decided to attend a short course. A few days later, I caught a train to Somerset. During that journey I read a textbook on pottery written by Bernard Leach who had been Michael Cardew's first teacher.

My pottery course was a relaxing break. Paul the potter met me from the train. He had a young family and they lived simple contented lives, deep in the countryside. The next day I had my first lesson on centring the clay on the wheel-head. For the next few days I was engrossed in learning to throw. By evening I would climb onto a borrowed bicycle and pedal to my lodgings for supper and bed, head still whirling from the hours I had spent staring at the rotating wheel.

By the end of my course, I had managed to make a few heavy, grotesque pots. The main thing I had learnt in Somerset was that I knew very little about pottery, but what I knew I loved.

By the time I returned to Kaduna, the building of the pottery was well under way. We were fortunate that a British lecturer from nearby Ahmadu Bello University had agreed to build us a two-chambered wood kiln. He had at one time worked with Michael Cardew in Abuja.

He was very keen and slaved in the hot sun, day after day, hardly stopping to rest or eat. Eli and I joined in whenever possible. Nothing would be imported for this pottery - kiln bricks, shelves and saggars were all made on the site - this was no mean task. Many helpers were recruited from nearby villages. Clay was dug out of the ground, soaked and sifted, in preparation for throwing pots.

Eli, guided by an architect friend, started building a

large oblong workshop using the local ironstone rock and mud. Instead of windows there were slits, shaped like arrowheads. There was no electricity on the farm at that time. Villagers assisted our farm workers to make some round houses with steep thatched roofs. These would be used for storing materials; the largest was to be a shop. Firewood was gathered from the bush and stacked neatly under a shelter close to the kiln. Lorry loads of grass were purchased from nearby farms and our Tuareg guards spent hours squatting under a shady tree, weaving the stems in preparation for thatching. It would be a race to complete the thatching before the rains started.

In this serene atmosphere the pottery took shape, and by 1983 the first pots were thrown and fired.

After the first firing, it took two days for the kiln to cool. Simon broke away the mud covering the doorways and pulled out the bricks. We all peered into the chamber. It was a perfect firing. Beer mugs, vases, decanters and jugs were unloaded. It had been like opening Aladdin's Cave. Our workers gathered around, gasping with delight and clapping as saggars were opened and shining pots removed. Simon could not wait to throw more pots.

One cool evening, Eli and I sat under the stars. We were firing the kiln and I had prepared a picnic supper. The pottery and farm were twenty kilometres away from town. It was a clear night with myriads of stars; the fresh scent of the wild ginger flowers was intoxicating. We could hear the weird call of nightjars as they flew across the valley. This romantic place, steeped in natural beauty was our heavenly retreat - but it had no name.

Eli sighed contentedly. 'Let's call it the Garden of Eden.'

I disagreed. His suggestion was far too biblical for my liking and it reminded me of serpents. I shuddered at the thought of the spitting cobras that had recently eaten the baby ducklings down on the farm.

I thought about our children away in England. They would love the pottery. I hoped they would soon return to live in Nigeria. One day all this would be theirs. Joe ...Caroline ... Andy. In a flash I thought of the name 'Ja - Car - Anda. 'Let's call it the Jacaranda.' Eli seemed pleased about our new name and planted Jacaranda trees around the perimeter of the farm. They eventually grew tall and during the dry season the purple blossom of the Jacaranda delighted many visitors.

Six months after the opening, Simon announced that he would be leaving us. We had not quarrelled, but his brother, a bank manager had offered him a loan to start a pottery in his home state. I was shocked when he told us because I did not know how I would run the pottery without him. We had recruited some hard-working Gbagi villagers and Simon had been training them, but they had not yet learnt how to throw. I appealed to Simon to stay for the rest of the year but his mind was set and he left early one morning without even saying good-bye.

'What an ungrateful fellow ... we built the Jacaranda Pottery for him,' I moaned to Eli.

He shrugged, quite unperturbed. 'Stop worrying, you'll easily find another potter - probably someone far better than Simon. Why don't you go to the University and look for a graduate?'

I had been invited to the 'end of year' exhibition in the Fine Arts Department of Ahmadu Bello University. There I met a vivacious lady potter whose work was stunning. Her name was Jokay and she needed a job. Jokay was an excellent potter with tremendous enthusiasm; she trained many workers and increased production. Soon we needed to expand and build more kilns. Gas was cheap and easy to use so we added some gas kilns. We had boreholes for water and bought a generator so I was able to introduce machinery. I visited Britain and returned with electric wheels and a pug mill.

Visitors urged us to build a small restaurant, where they would be able to take refreshments after visiting the pottery. The Jacaranda was a place of natural beauty far from the bustle and traffic of town. Andrew had just qualified in Hotel Management and Catering, and when he returned to Nigeria he was enthusiastic to run the restaurant. Together with Eli, he worked on the gardens and planted many rare blossoms and flowers. It was soon clear that Andrew had a flare for landscaping. He created a waterfall that trickled into a series of ponds full of goldfish and water lilies. The water attracted many rare birds. He grew orchids close to the cascading waterfall. The lowest pond contained crocodiles.

We rescued animals from traders and soon had a menagerie of antelopes, duikers and giant tortoises. The large male tortoise appropriately named Thumper would mount the female several times a day letting out loud rhythmic grunts. Of course the animals brought their own problems. One Sunday, a prosperous looking man brought his shy wife to the restaurant and Thumper started his usual antics, grunting loudly. The visitor took offence and ordered the waiter to intervene but, as this was physically impossible, he left in a huff. On another occasion our camel ate the Tuareg guard's baggy trousers.

Eli and I used to sit in the thatched breeze house

surrounded by colourful blossoms. Andrew's food was delicious, especially the large crispy prawns with garlic mayonnaise, Eli's favourite. Visitors came from other towns to buy Jacaranda pots and to sample the delicious food. Before long the Jacaranda Restaurant and Pottery were the talk of the town.

I continued to visit my mother frequently in Britain. Our youngest, Joe, was now reading law at Kingston, Surrey. In October 1986 I was staying in London with Caroline who was studying for her doctorate. I was meant to fly back to Nigeria the next day but I became ill, very ill. Eli was summoned from Nigeria and arrived as I was being wheeled into the theatre at the Cromwell Hospital in Kensington. The swift action of a brilliant surgeon saved my life. A few weeks later, using forceps, he dangled before me the eighteen inches of my perforated colon he had removed - he had preserved it in a jar of formaldehyde.

'You are a very lucky woman. I can't imagine what would have happened if you'd returned to Kaduna.' He had lived in Nigeria as a boy and was familiar with the poor hospital conditions there.

I had cheated death but it had been a lesson to me. Suppose I had died? What had I achieved in this world? It seemed unfair that life was so cheap in Nigeria, a country where people were dying because they could not afford basic hospital treatment. I had lain in that luxurious private hospital where food was served on silver trays. The cost of a disposable spittoon would have been sufficient to treat a child with malaria. Why should some lives be more valuable than others? Restless, I thought about the unfair values of this world. I knew I was searching for something, but did not know what.

I returned to my life at the Jacaranda where I was immensely happy. I had always admired traditional Nigerian pots and aimed to preserve this earthy quality and enhance rather than destroy an art that had existed in Africa for centuries. The generous round shapes of the local storage pots delighted me and I learnt to decorate them with carving and brushwork. Other potters came to the Jacaranda, stayed for a few months, and then left. Sometimes I invited potters from the old Abuja Pottery. They would throw and coil huge pots with traditional designs of tortoises, lizards, fish and snails. They loved our clay and were excited to use our equipment. I listened eagerly to their stories as they chattered about the wonderful old days in the Abuja Pottery with Michael Cardew.

As the time passed I began to spend more and more time at the Jacaranda, wandering around the farm with my dogs, decorating pots and talking to visitors. There was fun and laughter but we all worked hard to make Jacaranda special.

***

I had driven out to the Jacaranda Pottery earlier than usual, planning to glaze dozens of pots and load them into a kiln. Loading days were always busy, and I needed a full team so that we'd finish before dark. On that particular morning some of the key workers had not shown up. As I waited, my frustration and anger increased because I knew I couldn't manage without them. Where were they, I wondered? I guessed that they would eventually come with some paltry excuse. What would it be this time, illness, birth, or a burial? Esther, our shop assistant's words, rang in my ears.

'Gbagis are no good. They do whatever they like and they drink too much burukutu. They are so unreliable. Village and family always come first. They will attend every ceremony for miles around, and just don't care to work.'

I'd refused to heed her warnings and had continued to employ more Gbagis. I loved their humour and warmth but now I wondered if she had been right. I also knew that if a burial had kept them away, they'd fill themselves with burukutu. This strong local brew would knock out their pain but leave them hung over and wretched for days. 'Why are there always so many burials,' I grumbled to Esther, 'are so many people really dying or are they just using this as an excuse for a day off?' My anger was increasing, and my foot itched to kick over the stacked pots, but I remembered pottery wages would soon be due.

Esther tried to calm me. 'Take it easy Madam, there must be a real problem. It's the workers from Damisi village that are missing.'

At that moment a bicycle came into the compound. It was Danjuma, one of the absent potters. Before I could reprimand him, he blurted out, 'Drummer Boy is dead, we were there at his house all night, but the sickness was just too much. He died this morning.'

My anger was replaced by sadness and then regret. I knew Drummer Boy so well. He was about twelve years old, and used to hang around the pottery. Sometimes we'd give him small tasks, but he was much too young to be serious. Most of the time he would beat his drums and sing, how we all loved that. He would also share my biscuits. I should have done more for him. Now it was too late. The finality of death is always a shock, but when a child dies, the anguish cuts deeper. 'What was wrong with him? He was here the day before yesterday, and seemed fine?'

Danjuma shrugged, 'I only know that it was illness, the same one that carried away more that twenty children in Kakura Village last week. They complained of neck pain and headache and soon after they fell to the ground, dead.'

I felt a sudden compulsion to go to Drummer Boy's village. I needed to visit his family because Jacob, one of the absent potters, was his brother. I had always regretted that I knew very little about my workers and now I wanted to understand them better. How did they live? Were they really as poor as they made out? Was I misjudging them over their unreliable habits? 'Danjuma, will you go to his village with me? How far is it?'

'It will take almost an hour in the Land Rover - can you really drive there? The road is very rough?'

My mind was already made up. I wanted to meet these secluded people. Without wasting time we set off towards Damisi Village.

We drove along the main road and then turned off into the scrub, following a dusty cattle track. There were thorn bushes everywhere and they scratched the sides of the vehicle. Sometimes the track disappeared completely and massive termite-hills obstructed our way. We came to a dry streambed with steep rocky sides, and as I tried to accelerate, the truck tilted at a tantalising angle. I realised that some of my workers had to trek this route to work. No wonder they always seemed so lethargic.

The midday sun was glaring and scorching the earth. We jolted along and a herd of Fulani cows was startled by the appearance of the truck. They scattered in all directions and their calves galloped away, throwing their tails upwards like cobras. Vultures abandoned the offal they were scavenging and soared. A dust devil danced across our path gathering up dried leaves and sand, and then whirled away. Eventually we approached a cluster of huts, nestling together like a clumps of toadstools. I became aware of voices and waving hands and a blur of nakedness. We stopped abruptly and clambered out. There was the smell of smoke mingled with the odour of sweat. People began touching and greeting me. Adam, Jacob and other potters were there.

Adam led me into a mud hut where, in the darkness, as my eyes gradually adjusted, I saw Drummer Boy's thin body lying on a bamboo bed. The pallor on his face created a luminosity that emphasised the sharp angle of his jawbone. Meningitis, that dreaded illness of the hot dry season, had come into Damisi village and stolen this child. As I left the hut I noticed two small drums lying in the doorway.

I tried to express my sympathy to his blind father but words failed, so I just held his dry, claw-like hand. He stood there so thin and forlorn, dressed in tattered clothes. There outside in the blinding sunlight, children started to crowd around me, curious to see a baturia or white woman. Some were very frightened and ran screaming to their mothers. I stood staring at their terrible poverty.

Adam showed me his numerous children. They all had potbellies and gingery hair, synonymous with malnutrition. I noticed some were scratching their arms and legs, and looking closer I saw that they had scabies. The scratching in some cases had drawn blood. Flies buzzed around their bare legs, ulcers exuded pus. Some infants who hobbled towards us were deformed with rickets. The toddlers were completely naked, but the older children wore tattered clothes.

Jacob emerged from a nearby house and stumbled towards us looking drunk. Could this really be his home, because it didn't appear to be habitable? Part of the grass roof was missing and the walls were collapsing. I wondered why he hadn't renewed the thatch or patched the broken mud walls. It was obvious that his children were starving. Their spindly legs could hardly support their balloon-like bellies. Chronic ringworm infection on their scalps left shiny bald patches. Their sores oozed with pus and flies swarmed over their faces making for the eye corners. I was sure that none of these children had been immunised and it was inevitable that soon more lives would be lost. I realised that an injection costing only a few pence would save them.

I didn't wait to see Drummer Boy's body laid to rest in the shallow grave close to the walls of his house. Gbagis believe that the spirits of their dead stay close by until eternity.

By sunset, frenzied dancing and drumming would start. I noticed dozens of terracotta kegs of burukutu lying in the shade of a mango tree.

Driving back home, my mind jumping about like a frog in a pot, I thought of long-term plans but I also knew that I would have to act fast to stop the rapid spread of meningitis. On that journey back I knew that I was ready to devote my time to giving these children a better quality of life. Reflecting over the years I lived in Nigeria, I now realise that the voluntary organisation I had started to think about that day eventually became my life's most fulfilling work. During the years that followed I felt contented because I believed in what I was doing.

It was rather an anticlimax to find my husband resting

when I burst into the sitting room.

'Eli, you must wake up and listen because I have so much to talk to you about. Drummer boy died and I went to Damisi to sympathise. You know that he was Jacob's brother? Well, I was shocked to see the state of those village children. They were so wretched and full of illness and kwashiorkor.'

Eli's reaction was agonisingly slow. He'd obviously had a hard day at his clinic. I was almost reaching boiling point when he asked, 'Do you know what caused the boys death?'

'Yes. I'm certain it was meningitis. The illness was so sudden. He was playing at Jacaranda only two days ago. His brother told me that at least twenty children already died in one village close to Damisi. They had all complained of stiff necks and headaches.'

Eli frowned. 'Did you find out if those children had ever been immunised?'

'Adam says they haven't. They live so far from the main road. Government workers would never be able to visit such an isolated spot and I didn't see any health facilities there. Their village is utterly impoverished. Those children won't have any resistance to disease and I'm sure they'll all die if we don't act quickly.'

'You're probably right about the meningitis. We had two cases at the clinic this morning. It seems to be a bad year. I could spare Isa, our theatre nurse. He's very experienced and speaks Gbagi. He used to work in rural primary healthcare when he was with the government. He's the best person to send there and I can let him go with you tomorrow. You'll need to collect the meningitis vaccine and disposable syringes, and you'd better take along some worm medicine and multivitamins.'

Eli made a telephone call to our clinic and spoke

directly to Isa. Everything was arranged for the morning.

Isa was enthusiastic about working in Damisi village, and undaunted by its remoteness and rugged inaccessibility. He was knowledgeable about Gbagi people and chatted about their superstitions. Advising me about tackling healthcare in these isolated villages, he warned: 'We must first take permission from the chief, before we give any immunisation. If we upset the chief, there will be big palaver.'

When we entered the village, there was an eerie quiescence. I deduced that the villagers were hung over from the rituals of the previous night. Soon Adam emerged from his house frowning and telling us that two more children had died during the night. We could hear a distant wailing of women's voices and realised how imperative it was to start work immediately, so I said to Adam, 'We have no time to waste, would you take us to your chief?'

He shook his head. 'Our chief doesn't live here. He has a house back on the main road and has no interest in us, except when it is time to collect taxes. He's greedy for money so we don't see him often in these parts.'

At that moment a man appeared, riding a half-lame horse. He shouted to Adam who immediately prostrated himself on the dusty ground. The man wore a faded pink scarf tied around his fez and his flowing gown was shredded at the hem, as if his horse had bolted through thorn bushes. He dismounted using Adam's back as a stepping-stone. What pompous behaviour... his arrogance astounded me. The horse stood, head drooping, bony pelvis protruding through moth-eaten skin.

As Isa bowed, he whispered, 'Madam, this is the Chief of Damisi.'

'Good Lord!' I whispered. But I was relieved that he'd turned up, just in time.

After several moments of greeting, flattering and paying respects, we were able to get the support for immunisation and eventually were permitted to unload our cold boxes. As we did this, the chief squatted under a mango tree.

Adam entered several thatched houses, calling the occupants to come for injections. He dragged out some screaming children, and eventually a few nervous looking women emerged. He giggled as he explained that they were terrified of the needle. The chief growled at them to come forward but they stubbornly stood rooted to the ground.

Suddenly I had a brainwave. 'Give me an injection! I'm sure that will do it.'

Isa looked relieved, opened the cold box unloaded the syringes and the vials. He then drew up the vaccine rather ostentatiously and asked the women to gather round. Carefully swabbing my arm, he plunged in the needle. I managed to keep smiling, as the vaccine penetrated. The women were studying my face intently, then looked at each other and silently formed a line.

It was essential to keep records of the children's ages, but the mothers seemed confused and argued loudly amongst themselves. Was Audu born the year the river flooded? No, it was the time a strong wind ripped off their thatched roofs. Was Mary only a year old? Impossible! Her younger sister was already walking. To save time we decided to assess their ages.

Extracting the names of small babies proved even more impossible as the mothers just stood there smiling coyly. At first I thought they were acting stupidly until Isa explained. 'They believe that pagan gods will steal their child, if the name is spoken aloud.'

We therefore decided to jot down the mother's name, followed by a brief description - boy of six months with huge hernia - twins, three months, one large and one small - boy one month, pointed ears. Meanwhile, the queue started to lengthen.

I couldn't help giggling when the older children gave their names: Selection, Conception and Pentecost - these were their Christian names. The innocence portrayed on their wizened little faces did not mislead me for long and I saw one impish child slide a thrusting praying mantis down the neck of his daydreaming companion. There were peals of laughter as they teased and jostled in the queue until an occasional resounding slap delivered by a shrieking mother quenched high spirits for a short while.

In spite of their profound deprivation, these were the world's children, each one an important little being, with every right to a better quality of life. Adrenalin flowed through my veins. I had only one thing in mind: I would start a primary health care programme for the children of Damisi.

***

Our roving clinic to Damisi became a weekly event, crowded with Gbagi women and children, but the nomadic Fulani remained aloof and observed us with an air of scepticism. I sensed their distrust and felt saddened that their beautiful infants were left unprotected from infectious diseases.

I would load my Land Rover with medical supplies to treat common complaints like malaria, dysentery, coughs and colds but the demand increased rapidly as news about our mobile clinic spread to surrounding villages. Before long our team was seeing over a hundred infants each week. The villagers worked together to build a small round, thatched house in Damisi - this was their health-centre - we furnished it with a table and chairs. I recruited more nurses, and my pottery workers Humphrey and Esther volunteered to help. I employed an excellent driver, more as a precaution, because punctures and breakdowns occurred frequently.

In those early months Eli supplied all the medicines free, knowing that the villagers were too poor to pay. Unfortunately some babies were desperately ill and needed hospitalisation. Our private clinic back in town was soon overflowing with village children. Our staff referred to them as the Jacaranda Children. I was becoming addicted to the work; playing golf and going to parties were no longer on my agenda. I felt an inner strength and sense of fulfilment only interrupted when the children were too ill to be saved.

The worst killer was sickle cell anaemia, an illness so severe that it sometimes caused heart failure. Lifeless babies would be carried for miles to our clinic; repeated bouts of malaria and hookworm infestation had reduced their blood almost to water; their bellies were bloated due to starchy food and worms. Their survival in such an isolated village was unheard of. We perpetually rushed children to our hospital, but sometimes it was too late. Blood tests for HIV were always needed, but the Gbagi people were uneducated and afraid to donate their blood. Worn out mothers, arms entwined around their feverish babies, occupied our beds, whilst anxious relatives lolled about in the corridors. Unsanitary habits such as peeing and spitting greatly displeased our matron. Eli had always been generous and had never turned these children away but the situation was getting out of hand and our regular paying patients started to complain. The matron, who was Eli's younger sister, arrived at our house one morning, wringing her hands and frowning. I sensed trouble. She made a beeline for Eli who was having his breakfast. After a soft-toned greeting, she came to the point:

'Look at what happened last night. Imagine it! The controller of the Central Bank needed admission in our clinic and there was no bed for him. I moved the Jacaranda Children into a side ward to make space, but he had dysentery. Every time he needed the lavatory, those village people were using it. He packed his bag and left in a terrible rage, saying that in future his bank would use a different clinic.'

My husband looked rather put out and after she left he said, 'Margaret, you'll have to be reasonable about this. Try to make other arrangements for the village children. What about the General Hospital? We simply can't go on like this. *We* have to exist and at this rate all our regular patients will leave. We're not *missionaries* and I can't keep paying for their blood transfusions and medicines. I don't want to worry you but do you realise I can't even pay our salaries this month?'

I felt sick with worry knowing how Eli had worked for years to establish our private clinic that I was now ruining. I promised to make other arrangements, but then another child would come, feverishly gasping for breath. No time to waste - no choice - just this time - we can't leave this child to die. Nurses and doctors continued working and struggling against all odds.

Despairingly I visited the Ibrahim Abacha Children's Hospital, hoping for help. Ironically this hospital had been named after the son of a corrupt military dictator who had greedily bled the nation's purse dry.

The medical officer in charge knew how poor the Jacaranda Children were, but unfortunately medical fees weren't under his control and his hard-faced matron was unbending. However tragic the circumstances, she insisted on full payment before treatment would start. After hours of unnecessary waiting, our babies would be admitted to a ward, sometimes in close contact with cases of whooping cough, measles and chicken pox. These children of Damisi were already starving and had little resistance to infectious diseases; I began to feel that their admission was like a death warrant. I despaired for help.

One day Isa left me in Damisi as he had to rush back to town with a sick child. I was just packing up to leave when an old woman hobbled towards me, a woman like an ancient yew tree. A worn hand-woven cloth was wrapped around her waist but in spite of the biting harmattan wind her chest was bare, skinny breasts hanging like empty pouches. She seemed agitated, shook my arm and pointed to some huts. Adam indicated that I should follow her as she struggled over the rough ground supported by a long stick.

Entering the mud hut, Adam shooed away some chickens that flapped and squawked hysterically, raising clouds of dust. The fumes from a small charcoal brazier increased the fug and I started to choke.

A sick child lay on a mat. The head looked like a skull with deep eye sockets and prominent teeth. I pulled back the blanket and saw a boy's body. The old woman knelt down and seemed to be pleading with me.

Adam explained, 'She's his grandmother and she's

begging you to take him to the clinic.' Women were gradually crowding inside the hut and whispering. Then there was silence and they just stared at me.

I was almost crying, but took a tight grip - my upbringing didn't allow an exhibition of emotion. Softly I asked, 'How did he get into this terrible state? He's starving. Where are his parents?'

Adam explained, 'He's an orphan. We've tried to feed him, but he vomits everything. Our grandmother has tried to take care of him but she believes he's cursed. Most of his family are dead.'

I thought of Aids but felt sure that this dreaded disease hadn't reached such a remote village. I turned to Tony, my driver, who was shuddering in dismay.

'Go and bring some powdered milk from the Land Rover.' I felt reluctant to carry this boy to town as I assumed he was too ill to survive. Handing the old grandmother a few coins I advised her to buy some beans and eggs but deep inside I knew that this wouldn't help.

'Let's get going, it'll soon be dark.' I said as I walked away towards the Land Rover, turning my back on the grandmother. I pushed my guilt aside.

Tony started the engine and we drove away from the village. He spat through the open window as if to rid his body of the diseased village. For a while, I was unable to speak because I had failed to help a dying boy and my conscience was in pain. Then I could bear it no longer: 'Stop, Tony.'

He drew up under a baobab tree looking perturbed. 'What's happening? It's getting late, Doctor will be worried about you.'

'I know all that but I need to think. If I take this boy

to hospital he could die, then what will happen?'

'We'd have to bring his body back for burial. He's an orphan so that wouldn't be a problem.'

Grimly I weighed up the situation. I wouldn't be able to sleep in my bed that night if I left him there. I couldn't abandon him like that. 'Turn around, we're going back.'

A look of astonishment crossed Tony's face and then, sounding alarmed, he warned, 'Our petrol's very low - we'll never make it to the main road before the filling stations close. We'll be stuck.'

'I know all that, just drive.'

We rushed back to Damisi where Adam was still standing despondently outside the old woman's hut. He looked perplexed to see us return. 'Have you come for Tanko?'

I nodded as the villagers surrounded us and the grandmother hobbled out. Now I had become deeply involved and there was no turning back. 'I'll take him but he's very ill and I don't think there's much hope. If he dies will you blame me?'

The people exchanged glances and spoke together in hushed tones, then Adam said, 'They ask you to take him. He'll die in any case.'

Adam swathed Tanko's body in a cloth and passed him up to me in the Land Rover. As we headed for home, his head lolled against my arm and his ghost-like body seemed weightless, every rib and vertebra protruding. His brown hair was matted with filth and when his eyes opened, they floated up into his skull as he slipped in and out of consciousness.

Somehow we reached home and Tony carried him into our living room where my husband was anxiously waiting.

'Where have you been? Supper was ready hours ago. I

was about to come and search for you.' Then he saw the bundle my driver was carrying.

'What have you got there? Oh no, Margaret! What have you done this time?'

I sat Tanko on a cushion and holding him up, gently removed his vest. His spine looked like a column of cotton reels balanced precariously without support. His balloon-like belly protruded pushing against a bony cage of ribs. His neck seemed too slender to support his head. He opened his eyes and stared at Eli who said, 'Give him some Lucozade, he's very dehydrated.' As he slowly sipped, Eli took his stethoscope and listened to his heart whilst I took the temperature. Then Eli felt his bulging abdomen. 'His liver is grossly enlarged and he's very jaundiced. Look at his yellow eyes. The prognosis is poor.'

For a few moments Tanko seemed to have revived but a moment later, he retched and vomited up the putrid contents of his entire stomach. Eli phoned for our ambulance and we took him to our clinic for tests and a Darrow's Drip.

***

It was becoming impossible to handle the hundreds of children attending roving clinics, so to relieve the pressure I decided to open a second clinic at the Jacaranda Pottery. I fitted an empty thatched house with a sink, cupboards and a small refrigerator for our vaccines. This became our base camp, but the roving clinic was still vital because it reached out to those isolated people, steeped in superstition, who knew little about immunisation.

One morning in Damisi Village, a handsome boy called Sunday was brought for immunisation. His father was the schoolmaster from Kakura, a village more remote than

Damisi. I noticed his legs were abnormally bowed: as he stood in front of me the profile of his curved legs was like a hoop, his knees were at least two feet apart and the bones were abnormally flattened. He'd never be able to run or play football but still smiled. Feeling his flattened tibia, I said to Isa, 'Surely this can't be rickets? He looks well-nourished, his skin is glossy and there is no shortage of sunshine here.' Isa looked puzzled too.

'We'll give him some cod-liver oil,' I suggested, 'that'll help.' I counted out his capsules, surprised that his father, who was more educated than most villagers, seemed unperturbed by his son's deformity.

Then he spoke, 'There's one village called Kaffari where nearly all the children have this disease - my wife grew up there. There's no cure.'

Another man waiting in the queue for vaccination added, 'Telele and Pam Madaki's children have this same problem only their legs are much worse.'

Without giving the matter much thought I replied, 'I'd like to see them. Would they be able to come to Jacaranda next week? We'll give them some medicine.' Later that night as I prepared the drug requisition, I added a few extra bottles of cod-liver oil to the list.

The next clinic was at the Jacaranda and it ran smoothly. As the red sun sunk into the harmattan dust, we finished work and were ready for home, but the farm gates clattered open and a procession of young children appeared, hobbling and staggering from side to side like little trolls, their determined faces showed they were bent on reaching me. At least thirty children limped through the gates; some used sticks while others were carried. Many crowded into the hut and looked searchingly into my eyes, with eager expressions as if they believed that I could cure them. The sight of their gross deformities came as a shock and I studied them first with horror and then with great sadness. They had unusually square heads that contributed to their gnome-like appearance. Their short stature was due to their grossly deformed legs, as if the bones had been smashed with a sledgehammer and then twisted and dislocated into grotesque shapes. Some knees faced sideways or knocked together, others were so acutely bowed that balance was impossible. A few crawled over the stony ground wearing kneepads cut from old tyres. One little boy smiled up at me and offered his deformed hand and I took it, studying his earnest expression and asked him in Hausa language, 'What's your name?'

'Nehemiah.' He then pointed to two smaller boys, both unable to walk and supported by their father. 'He's Gideon and this is Ahila.'

Hiding behind their father's baggy trousers, a pretty little girl peered at me timidly - she was called Mariamu. These children radiated an aura that drew me close to them.

A thin, serious man introduced himself as the chief of Telele. He was very humble and so different from the chief of Damisi. He pleaded, 'Can you help us? We don't understand why our children are like this - when they are babies their legs are straight, but when they start to walk, their legs bend like wind-beaten rice.' He eased a small boy nearer and added, 'This is Dogara, my youngest child. He can't run and will never be able to farm when he grows up.' I noticed tears in the chief's eyes and realised how deeply he treasured his son. Dogara gazed at me, his bright face full of hope.

'How far is your village from here?' I asked.

The Chief waved his arm towards some distant hills. 'We have been walking since early morning.'

Feeling responsible that I had raised their hopes - to disappoint these children would have been unthinkable - I racked my brain over how best to handle the situation. I hadn't brought nearly enough cod-liver oil and couldn't send the children home with nothing.

There was a sudden wave of excitement as Eli's twenty-year-old Mercedes rattled up the slope from the farm. He'd been working in his orchard, grafting mango seedlings. As Eli climbed out, many of the children, who were unfamiliar with cars, touched the paintwork and discovered the mirrors. They peeped at themselves and pulled funny faces, started laughing and shoved others to have a go.

'Are you coming home Margaret?' Then Eli saw the deformed children and frowned. 'Good heavens! Where have they all come from? I haven't seen anything quite like this before.'

'I'm so relieved you've come! Look at these children, what's wrong with them?' I asked. 'Is it rickets?'

Eli frowned and examined one extreme case. 'This one looks more like the 'sabre' limbs typical of tertiary syphilis, but they're far too young for that. It's a rickets type of disease, but I wonder what's causing it? '

Isa and Eli examined the children, talked to their parents and we handed out most of our medicines. The cod-liver oil wasn't enough, so I gave them multivitamin syrups and worm medicine, promising that we'd try to bring more cod-liver oil next time. The boot of Eli's Mercedes was crammed with tangelos, so we shared them amongst the children who wasted no time in tearing off the peel and vigorously sucking out the juice.

I realised that it would soon be dark and asked Eli, 'How are we going to get them back to their villages? Some look absolutely exhausted and apparently it took them hours to trek here.' I spotted our drivers, Sylvester and Tony, standing in the shade.

Eli beckoned to them. 'Go and bring both tipper lorries from the farm and make sure they're clean.' A few moments later the lorries lurched up the farm track and the children's excitement became almost uncontrollable. Sylvester used a small ladder and one by one Tony lifted the excited children up onto the back of the lorries. It was a struggle to load so many on board but soon the lorries were crammed full. We promised the chief of Telele that we'd visit him to try to find out the cause of the abnormalities. The children couldn't believe their luck and as the tippers drove off they waved and clapped and started singing. Eli, Isa and I watched silently. We were deeply moved because, in spite of their disablement, these children were so full of joy. The three of us agreed to help but the question was, how to begin?

***

Eli had been appointed to various governing bodies in Nigeria and frequently travelled to meetings far away from Kaduna. I always dreaded being left alone at night because violent armed robberies were on the increase. Conversation at dinner parties would lapse into hushed accounts of the latest horrors. We both assumed that our turn would eventually come; our thick metal bedroom door would be useless against marauders armed with ex-military sub-machine guns. We both agreed that whatever happened, we'd put up a fight, rather than face torture and humiliation.

That morning Eli was going for a meeting in a town called Minna about a hundred miles away. He was the chairman of the board of trustees of the Ibrahim Babangida Specialised Hospital. It was during that military dictator's regime that corruption had escalated in Nigeria. Now there were plans to privatise this extravagant medical centre. It was just another white elephant: its over-elaborate design and sophisticated equipment with central air conditioning required a regular supply of electricity and water, unheard of in those parts. Once Julius Berger, the German contractors, had handed it over, skilled engineers to maintain the equipment were unobtainable locally and hospital admission fees were unaffordable to many poor Nigerians. The general lack of good medical facilities throughout Niger State had made life difficult for the underprivileged. Frustrated over the lack of funding to maintain this hospital, Eli had to journey once again along the dangerous highway for another meeting. He was fully aware that government would probably not heed the professional advice of the board members but he still supported his backward state and would never abandon his ideals. He spoke sadly about this sinful waste of money that could have been used to build at least twenty practical health centres in rural areas.

Before Eli drove from our compound, he promised to speak to one skilled orthopaedic surgeon who worked there in Minna; at least he would get advice about treating grossly deformed children who suffered from rickets.

***

126

I had been told that there was a brilliant English paediatrician in the Ahmadu Bello Teaching Hospital in Kaduna. This lady doctor was busy in the children's ward and I felt guilty for intruding but I'd been advised that this was the only way to speak to her, as she was always too overworked to give appointments.

That day the ward was overflowing with ill children and extra mattresses lined the outside corridors where there was a foul stench from an open drain. Flies swarmed everywhere so I made for the doorway hoping for some fresh air. Looking out over the hospital compound I noticed stained bed-sheets drying on the dusty ground. Beyond was an open space where a few people squatted, relieving themselves, oblivious to their surroundings. It had been raining in the night, but as the sun came out, the dampness rose and the foul stench of human faeces hung in the air. It seemed that there was insufficient working sanitation in this relatively new multi-million teaching hospital - basic human needs were not a priority.

A little later, the doctor came over to me, she was a young English woman. Apologising for interrupting I asked if she'd have a look at some photographs I'd taken of the rickets. I explained that I'd been giving the children cod-liver oil and wondered if this was the best thing to do? She glanced at the pictures and said confidently, 'You're quite right. This is a rickets type of disease, but you could drown the kids in cod-liver oil and it wouldn't help them because their bodies are unable to break down vitamin D into an absorbable form. I see children like these all too frequently. The drug calciferol usually helps and I always bring a supply back from my UK leave. It's hard to get here and very expensive.'

My hopes were rising as I could picture raising money

to buy massive supplies of this drug. 'What exactly is calciferol?'

'It's an absorbable form of vitamin D. If children prone to rickets could have it early in life, it would prevent them from developing these deformities and it could also arrest this deteriorating condition in young children who are already affected.'

'How do you administer it? Is it in tablet form or by injection?'

'Either, but the children's level of calcium must be closely monitored. Too high a dose can lead to kidney complications later on.'

I realised how difficult it would be to monitor dozens of children living scattered over such remote areas. 'Do you know the root cause of this illness?' I asked hopefully.

'It seems to be linked with the mother's genes. Some women are more prone than others. Something is triggering it off, maybe a toxic substance; it would be an interesting project for research but, as far as I know, nothing much has been done so far.' Our brief discussion ended abruptly when an agitated nurse rushed forward

'Doctor, come quickly! Baby Hassan is convulsing!'

Walking back to my car, deep in thought, I was conscious of a woman walking towards me along the narrow veranda. It was probably her irregular steps that first drew my attention and then she seemed to stagger. Just as I passed, she squatted and tugged open her wrapper. I heard her moan and a slimy grey bubble, like a balloon, dropped onto the path.

At first I stood there mesmerised and then stooped to peer. The bubble moved so I instinctively pulled its membranes apart. Through the clear birth fluids I noticed a tiny pink leg, toes fanning wide, kicking and thrusting as if in anger. Next an elbow appeared, followed by a hand with a perfect set of finger-nails. I hastily dragged the rest of the membrane away and saw a beautifully formed head with black curls. Some nurses came and attended to the placenta - and as I gathered the tiny mite up it started to roar. I placed him in his mother's arms, inwardly smiling over the generous size of his manhood. Another tiny human had just crash-landed to earth to begin the journey along a crooked road.

The next day I set off for Telele Village with Tony my driver and the two Gbagi potters, Adam and Danjuma, who were to act as interpreters. As we drove out of the farm gates some of the Gbagis waved us off. We soon left the tarred road and joined a narrow winding track that lead deep into the bush. It was early rainy season and the road was muddy from the previous night's downpour. Thorny bushes boxed us in and occasionally scraped against the side windows. Adam and Danjuma leaped out of the vehicle, machetes in hand to hack away the tough branches obstructing our route. Startled birds flew out, shrieking in fright; we passed trees alight with scarlet blossoms, haloed by bees.

Soon, we reached a clearing where the soil was dark and fertile. Mushroom shaped black termite hills were dotted everywhere, quite different from the usual red steeple shaped forms. Men and women, stripped to the waist, were hoeing the ground. Their jet-black bodies dripped with sweat and glistened in the scorching sun. At first they seemed mesmerised by the sudden appearance of our Land Rover and then they waved and shouted greetings. Adam seemed to know everyone along the route and shouted through the open windows, laughing good-naturedly and exchanging news.

After a few miles, the track seemed to disappear as the ground became rocky. Tony steered the Land Rover up a bare granite face and as we climbed. the engine struggled against the gradient. I was relieved to reach the summit and we all clambered out onto the boiling rocks and stared at the rich landscape below. Through the trees I could see small clusters of thatched houses and in the distance were herds of cattle being driven towards a stream that meandered across a plain. There was a wisp of smoke rising like a taut thread through the still air and I traced it down to a cluster of domed wattle houses. These were the temporary dwellings of the nomadic Fulani.

We could hear some cattle bellowing and the distant sound of a Gbagi drum. Vultures circled over our heads, gliding in the currents of air, and flocks of Cordon Bleus, Fire Finches, Waxbills and other tiny birds tweeted and prattled in the thorny scrub. I wanted to linger in this natural paradise but we had to move on. The descent disturbed my peace because Tony mischievously took his foot off the brakes allowing the vehicle to race down the steep slope, rattling as it gathered speed, almost out of control.

Once again we joined our winding track, now bordered by shrubs, heavily laden with dangling green pods of beans, a staple food of the Gbagis. As we rounded another bend I saw dozens of granaries perched precariously on the sides of a rocky dome. They were round like giant mud pots with legs. Their small grass roofs tilting haphazardly created a comedy that reminded me of tubby little trolls, hats askew. These were storage vats for guinea corn, maize and millet, so essential to the village people. Chickens roosted in the shade and others pecked at some scatterings of grain. I knew we must be close to Telele.

We started to descend into a dark forested area where the track was muddy. Tony slammed on the brakes to avoid a deep gully that traversed our route. I stared in dismay and got out of the Land Rover, trying to decide what to do next. A short distance down stream was a wooden bridge consisting of a few splintered planks, knitted together with a rusty bicycle chain. On the sandy bank beneath were deep hoof prints overflowing with brown cows urine. I gingerly picked my way through the undergrowth and balanced on the bridge, wobbling nervously, noticing some women further downstream filling earthenware pots with this polluted water. At that moment a swarm of tsetse flies attacked me viciously, jabbing their proboscis through my tough jeans - a thousand burning injections. At that I leapt across the planks and squelched into a pile of slippery cow dung. Adam and Danjuma followed, trying to hide their amusement. At that moment Tony started the engine and drove the Land Rover straight towards the gully. It slid down the embankment, but the other side was much steeper. Revving the engine furiously he tried to climb the steep bank, but the vehicle slipped backwards into the streambed. Now he was stuck!

'What the hell do you think you're doing?' I asked furiously. 'You should have waited.' Tony acted deaf and hid his face behind the steering wheel. He shoved the gears into traction and tried again. This time the Land Rover climbed steadily but the incline was growing steeper, so he throttled and for one horrendous moment it seemed that the vehicle would roll over. With the nerve of the devil, he hung on, the Land Rover suspended at a terrible angle; he started to accelerate with so much force that I thought the engine would burst but, greatly to my amazement, it shot over the top of the embankment. There was a distinct smell of burning rubber as the smoking Land Rover came to rest on the other bank.

'Don't ever do that again. We could easily have trekked this last part. That was a crazy risk!'

I was furious and yet relieved to escape the tsetse bites. We drove on, passing women and children carrying large pots and buckets to collect water.

Then I saw Telele Village, a conglomeration of mud houses of all shapes and sizes, thatch roofs blending into a background of trees and rocks. In strong contrast stood an ugly half finished building of cement blocks and zinc pan roof, adorned with an oversized placard printed in blue, announcing 'The Assemblies of God Mission'. Close by was a large dilapidated mud building with the remains of a tattered roof of mouldy straw hanging down the walls. A bell startled us and soon dozens of children poured out through the doorway, followed by a man, waving a cane. Many of the children were deformed with rickets but still hobbled forward, excited at seeing us with our vehicle. The smaller infants, terrified of my white skin, howled and fled. The teacher greeted us and led us towards what I assumed was the chief's house.

We walked past two huge bulls tethered to a tree and entered a small courtyard where goats grazed on dried up guinea corn stalks. The children had already raced ahead so the chief was waiting outside his door, smiling, bowing and welcoming us warmly. He beckoned to some youths who went inside and heaved out a huge upholstered chair that they dragged under a baobab tree. This chair must have had an amazing history - it looked as if it had once belonged to Lord Lugard, who had been the Governor General of Northern Nigeria more than a hundred years before.

The chief proudly urged me to sit but I felt ill at ease because it would be like occupying his throne. A tray of warm coke tins was handed to us. The chief was genuinely delighted by our visit but I needed to see more of his village to find out why so many children had rickets, so we asked him to show us their drinking water. He led us to a well that was covered with a jagged piece of zinc. I peered down the dark shaft and dropped a small pebble, straining to hear a splash. It was at least eighty feet deep and the walls were crumbling. The chief's wife came to draw water, lowering a rubber pouch, made from an old inner tube and tied to a frayed rope. She emptied the well water into a white enamel bucket - it looked very dirty and smelt of frogs - not surprising because chickens and ducks scratched the surroundings, their droppings mingling with the spillages. I crinkled my nose up as the chief explained that a cobra had fallen into the water a few days before.

We moved on and entered the dilapidated school. There were neither doors nor windows - just openings. The walls were pitted and broken, and Tony pointed to a red scorpion, disguised and nestling there on the reddish mud walls. The roof had been torn away - probably by the wind - and the beams had been eaten by termites and were on the point of collapsing. The furnishing consisted of mud desks and benches. A tiny blackboard hung on the wall. Written on it were the words 'Jesus is Lord.'

All that remained was to administer oral polio to the children. The chief caringly sat beside me, holding each infant as I dropped the vaccine into its open mouth. The children were badly malnourished and their teeth were decayed, their gums were pale with anaemia. They were in an even worse condition than the children of Damisi.

I noticed the time and remembered the huge gully we had to cross and so we hurried to the Land Rover. The whole village came to see us off in a cacophony of farewells; their appealing expressions and warmth were too precious for words.

***

It was one of those rare mornings when the weather is perfect. Swallowtail butterflies were busily fluttering around the pink hibiscus while sunbirds hovered over the golden shower flowers, thrusting their tongues into the deep trumpets to suck up the nectar. The branches of the mahogany trees were alive with bird life. In the valley beyond our farm, I noticed a gentle wisp of smoke rising from the nomadic settlements, and I pictured the women frying tomatoes and peppers on an open fire. Some blue mountains stood out sharply from the plain. This was Africa at its best and my spirit was filled with joy.

At that moment, I heard the farm gates open and there was the sound of a vehicle, so I stopped daydreaming and made my way towards the workshops. Danjuma stood at the door, calling the potters to come and see our unexpected visitors.

'They're important people. Look, that's the Fulani District Head.' I was surprised to see quite a number of robed men clambering out of a mini-bus. This rather solemn procession approached me and I gave the traditional greeting. 'Sannu de Zuwa' - Welcome from your journey.

They replied, 'Salamu alaikum,' Peace be unto you.

Feeling reassured, I led them into a cool round hut and they quietly seated themselves in a ring. I wondered why they had come. One young man stared at me through black eyeliner and I gazed back at his red dyed lips and wondered if he was a eunuch. The scent of their civet-based perfume was strong. The elderly leader wore a blue flowing robe with a white turban. My potters were peeping through the windows and one whispered,

'Some of them are chiefs. Look at the old man - he's the chairman of the Maiyati Allah.' A handsome man clad in an embroidered white kaftan addressed me in well-spoken English.

'We've travelled far to bring you this message. We've come to condole you over the loss of your sister.' His words astonished me. How did they know that I had a sister? My sister and I rarely communicated and I wasn't aware of her death. Hoping that they were mistaken I said,

'My sister is well. I don't understand.'

They looked at each other and murmured amongst themselves. Their spokesman smiled knowingly. 'We heard about it on the radio - your sister, the princess.'

I was still perplexed and then understood. They'd hired this bus to travel miles to share in my sadness over the death of Lady Diana. Their quiet concern moved me deeply. We belonged to different worlds and yet this rush of warmth and affection flowed between us. Before they left, the chairman of Maiyati Allah told me that if ever I needed help, the Fulani would support me. His son whispered,

'He's a powerful man and will be true to his words.' Years later, I remembered his promise and wished he really could help me.

In the early years of Hope for the Village Child we had experienced irritating problems with the Fulani nomads. At that time their chiefs wouldn't allow their children to be vaccinated at our health clinics. Then one stiflingly hot day in Damisi Village when our health hut was overcrowded with

135

women and children, a group of Fulani appeared. The Gbagi people trusted us and attended clinics in multitudes and we'd managed to immunise most of their children. The Fulani women were more sceptical and their men-folk forbade them to have their babies immunised. But they were very inquisitive. Peering in through the small windows, their shrill voices made it hard for us to concentrate; the already airless hut was dark enough, without having the little existing light blocked out by their heads. Annoyingly, their men-folk drove their herds of cattle close to the hut, so the smell of dung and swarms of flies added to our discomfort. However irritated we felt, we would greet them cheerfully, hoping that one day we'd win their trust.

That day a Gbagi woman rushed in with a very ill child. 'He's been having fits. His fever has been high for several days.' She wept as she thrust the child towards me. I looked at the boy, whose small body was burning with fever. His short breaths were irregular and his heartbeat was tacky. I knew the family well, and baby Amos, usually notorious for his pranks, lay there, almost lifeless. I wondered why she had delayed seeking help for so long and said, 'He'll have to go to hospital right now. I hope he'll make it because he's terribly ill - go and get ready and hurry.'

I gathered up my belongings and was heading for the Land Rover when the dreaded sound of screaming was heard. She came running back along the path carrying Amos, who appeared dead. All the women in the hut started to wail and the agonised sound of grief filled the air. A huge crowd gathered, pushing their way forward. I seized the child and ran back to the hut where the nurses and I worked together. One nurse massaged the heart and another gave mouth-to-mouth resuscitation but there was no pulse and no respiration. Amos changed to a dark bluish colour. I didn't want to lose this precious mite. 'Come back Amos, please don't die. God save this lovely boy.'

Time stood still and it seemed so hopeless. In the meantime the Fulani at the window jumped back and were grouped. I understood that they were saying, 'Look what she's done. We told you so. You can't trust any of them.' I pumped the frail chest very hard and wondered if the force was too much. I thought he was gone but like a miracle he responded. First Amos stirred and then he cried out. This was followed by a fit. Our nurse was an expert at dealing with convulsions and injected whilst I tepid-sponged the thin body. The crisis was over and Amos gazed around, his big brown eyes staring in amazement. We carried him to the Land Rover and fled to the hospital.

He made a wonderful recovery and his grateful father couldn't stop thanking me. 'What can I do to repay you?' he asked. My request was modest.

'When you go back to your village, take Amos and show him to the Fulani; they still don't trust us.'

The Fulani brought all their girls to the next clinic for oral polio. A month later, they allowed their sons to come too but they still refused to have injections. Our progress was slow and we waited for several weeks. Then one day their chief asked why we only injected Gbagi children. For a brief moment I saw a twinkle in his eye and realised that though he was proud he was asking for help.

His son was the first Fulani to receive measles immunisation at our clinic. Gradually we earned their trust and they became our friends.

One Sunday morning when I was working in the Jacaranda, a woman rushed in, crying. She must have known that the tiny bundle on her back, her newborn baby, was already dead. By lunchtime, two more babies were brought to me - too late, they were also dead. I stared sadly at the still body of a baby girl, dressed in pink, like a tiny doll. They had all died of dysentery. I needed to act quickly to find out the cause of this disease. They had come from Kakura, a village beyond Damisi that had been the source of the worst cases of neglect and illness I'd seen during our roving clinics. The Damisi villagers had constantly advised me to keep away from Kakura, but were a superstitious lot. Now I wished I'd followed my gut instinct and visited that village.

'How far is Kakura?' I asked Adam the next day.

'Kakura … that's a big problem … there's no way you can go in your Land Rover.'

'There must be a route. How did those mothers reach our clinic?' Adam saw that I was determined to go and continued to dissuade me.

'Ma, it's not possible. During the dry season you can go by road, but at the moment the rains have caused the stream to flood, Kakura's cut off. There's a track that runs from Damisi, but it's very rough and the bushes are overgrown. Those people are full of juju. Ma don't go, leave it.'

But I'd made up my mind and nothing would deter me; if mothers with tiny babies could trek, then so could I.

I remembered that we possessed three motor-cycles donated by Unicef. My attempt to ride the lady's machine had failed. My first lesson had been going well and I was chugging around our compound, gradually gaining confidence, when I mistakenly pressed the throttle instead of the brakes and crashed heavily into the back of our parked tipper lorry. My boobs were bluer than a baboon's bum. The thump to my body, and worse still to my ego, had put me off ever trying again. However, time heals. I had to get back onto that motorbike again.

I chose Danjuma to be my 'chauffeur' as he was the most suitable of my workers, sensible and strong. I told him to take me to Kakura on the pillion. Humphrey and Isa came with us on the other bikes.

I hadn't journeyed on a motorcycle for years and found that there was nothing much to hold onto, except Danjuma's waist and I didn't want to embarrass him; I felt that I was going to lose my balance at any moment. It was a bumpy journey and I tried to ease my weight by holding the saddle. It didn't give much relief and shock waves jabbed through my spine. Leather boots and a thick drill safari suit gave little protection from the thorny branches.

It was beautiful - Africa can be so wonderful. A red flanked duiker ran across our path; later I noticed porcupine quills lying at the hollow base of a termite hill. Scarlet bishop birds perched on swaying branches, and red-breasted shrikes disappeared like ghosts into the luxuriant undergrowth. As we entered a forested area, there were orchids growing on gnarled tree trunks and bright red toadstools carpeted the moist ground. It was fascinating but there was also a weird aspect. A few bones hung from the trees, probably the remains of antelopes or sheep. Perhaps they were meant as a deterrent to strangers.

'Are we nearly there?' I asked Danjuma, who looked worried.

'No Ma, but we're more than halfway.' He pointed

towards a hill. 'That's Kakura hill. It's full of juju.' A granite hill rose out of the scrub like a canine tooth.

I started to laugh. There I was, sixty plus, riding a motorbike. At least I wouldn't meet any of my friends here.

Kakura was larger than I'd expected. There were dozens of thatched dwellings and the people crowded around and greeted us warmly. I was relieved to recognise some of our previous patients who were delighted to see me. Judging from their excitement, I wondered if a white person had ever visited Kakura. Then I noticed a dilapidated church, probably built years before by missionaries.

We visited the chief, an old blind man. He was toothless and slurped burukutu from a calabash. His hut stank like a local beer parlour. The pastor showed us around the village. The first thing I asked to see was their wells but the pastor frowned and shook his head.

'Every time we dig a well, it collapses. Just as the diggers are reaching water when the earth is soft, the sides cave in … last year two men were buried. Now we drink from the stream.' He showed us several unused wells, covered by a few spindly branches. I warned him to cover the holes before a child fell inside. He led us to a stagnant stream with dirty looking water.

'Do you boil this water before drinking it?' I asked.

'No. It was good enough for our grandparents. A thirsty man has to drink … no time to be boiling water.'

Earlier I had been told of their superstition. They believed that babies should not be breast-fed for the first three days of their lives because that early thick milk would harm them. Newborn babies were therefore given stream water.

With the help of interpreters, Isa and I tried to

140

enlighten the people about the danger of feeding babies with contaminated water. The elders listened and said they would never change their custom but they eventually agreed that their women should boil water to prevent more deaths.

The herbalist, a cantankerous man, seemed to despise any new ideas. The pastor must have thought I was their 'great redeemer', with funds unlimited, because as we were leaving, he asked me to build a school and health clinic. Probably because I was white, he believed that I was loaded with money. I, on the other hand, knew that one decent concrete lined well, with a cover and hand pump, would save many lives.

As we rode out of the village through a thickly wooded area, I heard a strange sound. We stopped to listen. It came from behind a tree, an uncanny wailing monotone. Humphrey and Isa went to investigate and I followed behind closely. When Humphrey reached the tree, he let out a shout, covered his eyes and ran back, nearly bumping into me.

'Ma, don't look, it's terrible.'

'What is?' I cautiously approached. Under the tree sat an adolescent girl. She had a tropical ulcer that extended from her knee to her ankle. It was so deep that her tibia bone was exposed, gleaming white, the surrounding flesh oozing with pus. It smelt foul and flies were plaguing the poor girl. I thought I would retch but smiled weakly whilst Isa talked to her. She was called Rifkatu and she said that her leg had been infected for seven years. She had become an outcast because her smell was so foul that the villagers could not take her into their homes. People would give her food but she had no shelter. Tactlessly I said to Isa, 'Surely her leg will have to be amputated. She'll die if it's left like that.' Rifkatu stood up and using a long stick hobbled away into the undergrowth. She must have understood my words because she no longer trusted me.

The memory of Rifkatu haunted me for days. At the first lull in the rains, I went back to search for her. She was hiding in the forest. I had made arrangements with an orthopaedic surgeon to treat her. It took time to win back her trust but eventually she agreed to come into town with us. I encased her diseased leg in a thick plastic bag, tied it tightly and with windows wide open, drove the Land Rover to hospital. I was silently repeating our motto, 'Nothing human is alien to me.' I prayed that I would endure the stench.

***

After the tragic deaths of those babies from Kakura, I began to realise that dysentery was rampant throughout most of the villages. Week after week the same children came to the clinic with recurrent diarrhoea. Polluted drinking water was the cause.

Another serious waterborne disease was polio. Feverish children from Togache and Kafari were carried to our clinic; days later, when the fever had subsided, their limbs were paralysed. Driving along the track to Togache I saw children struggling to walk, sometimes crawling, their limbs flapping uncontrollably. At that time vaccines were scarce but our nurses increased their efforts with immunisation, riding motorbikes to reach some of the more remote nomadic settlements.

This problem of polluted water weighed heavily on my mind and I decided to visit Sister Rosa, a nun who was very experienced in organising primary healthcare. She had become my friend, and never failed to give useful advice. Over the past months she had guided me, suggesting ways forward with the project. She always stressed the importance of educating the women and I saw that this was essential if we were to progress.

When I went to her office she was about to leave for a workshop, but I blurted out the problem and she sat down to listen. I could not conceal my anguish. 'The cases of dysentery are increasing. Some of the children have been re-infected so many times that they've become anaemic - some even develop heart failure. Unless these villages are provided with decent wells, the infant mortality rate will continue to rise.' I went on to describe the deaths of the newborns in Kakura.

Sister Rosa listened, pausing thoughtfully before she spoke. 'This is a tragic situation. Unfortunately it's what's happening in many rural parts of Nigeria. But I have an idea - there's a Dutchman called Theo Huitema - maybe he will help you - he's an expert. He has a team of workers but also trains the village youths to assist in building wells, lined with reinforced concrete rings and fitted with hand-pumps. These would be a big improvement. The only problem is that he's difficult to reach because most of the time he works in remote places.'

It seemed that a glimmer of light had broken through the fog. I wondered how much Theo Huitema would charge. For once we had funds, a donation from a company whose wives came from Abuja to buy pots. The women had occasionally arrived when the clinics were running and had been shocked at the poor condition of the babies. 'Will Theo Huitema be expensive? Do you think a hundred thousand naira would be enough?'

Sister Rosa was gathering her files to leave for her meeting: 'That would be a good start. Leave it with me. I'll try to locate him.'

As I drove to Jacaranda, I pondered over Sister Rosa's advice: 'Believe in what you are doing. Have you considered that worrying shows lack of faith?' I envied her outlook and realised that I had probably become cynical. I had witnessed suffering and diseases that would never be allowed to happen in Britain. I refused to believe that the life of a child in the west is more valuable than that of a child in the third world. I thought about the rapid progress with the children's health and marvelled over the unexpected donations that had sometimes appeared in times of greatest need. Sister Rosa's idea of faith was comforting. I would pin my hopes on Theo Huitema and could hardly wait to meet him.

The following Sunday, Eli invited Graham Quinne to join us for lunch. He was an interesting man and a brilliant agriculturist who had worked in Nigeria for years. Sadly he was nearing retirement ... he would be irreplaceable. After lunch we walked around the farm and Graham named the different varieties of mango trees. Eli mentioned that we needed to sink boreholes at the Jacaranda. Graham demonstrated how to dowse for water. He used two wire coat hangers bent into L-shapes and showed us how to grasp one in each hand. As I walked about holding my rods, they gradually swung together; then, as I continued to walk, the rods parted. I could hardly believe the force I was holding and was puzzled. Could I be influencing the rods subconsciously? I asked Eli to lead me about and I closed my eyes. Sure enough the rods swung together when Eli led me back to that same spot. Graham's eyes danced with delight. 'Not everyone can dowse. It's a wonderful gift.'

Days later I wandered about the farm, a rod in each hand, and gradually discovered how to trace the courses of underground streams. Little did I know how useful this would be in the coming months. The Gbagi potters believed it was juju and rejected my offer to teach them. They were scared to touch the rods.

It was during one immunisation clinic in Telele when I started my first real search for water. There had been no rain for seven months and the soil was parched. Dwellings, clustered together on a rocky outcrop, were without wells, and the women, like beasts of burden, were forced to trek to a stream to fill their kerosene tins. Herds of Fulani cattle drank from that stream, wading and urinating in the shallow water.

My friend Joy and her husband Reg happened to be visiting from England. She was vibrant and her name suited her. Joy always enjoyed seeing the villages because a few years before, she had been a VSO in the far north of Nigeria. During her Voluntary Service Overseas years, she had witnessed poverty in the rural areas, and although not well off, was always ready to help those in need, especially potters. During this particular visit, she had organised a national pottery exhibition, the first to be held in Nigeria. It had been a tremendous success.

I collected the divining rods from the car, held them horizontally and started walking. Joy, usually dead earnest, struggled to hide her amusement. 'You look as if you're sleep walking. No wonder the villagers see this as powerful juju.'

That day the rods did not respond even though I walked methodically up and down the slopes in a grid-like pattern. The daylight began to fade; there was no trace of water so I gave up.

The next morning I was determined to continue searching for water in Telele. Joy and I left home early, hoping to beat the rush hour. When we reached Sabon Tasha (usually called the 'Tanker Village) just five miles short of Jacaranda, there was a bad traffic hold-up. The deep potholes in the road were being patched and the smell of the hot tar and smoke permeated the air already thick with exhaust fumes. Dozens of tankers were lined up along the roadside, some tilted precariously as their wheels sunk into crumbling laterite. The narrow strip of tar that represented the main artery to the Kaduna Refinery was jammed with cars and taxis, blaring their horns. Young children threaded their way through this congestion selling hard-boiled eggs, grubby looking bread and fried batter-balls known as puff-puffs. Market vendors hauled carts laden with stems of bananas, yams, sweet potatoes and sacks of grain. Schoolchildren scuttled between vehicles and women burdened with firewood struggled towards the market.

The traffic police, nicknamed Yellow Fevers because of the colour of their jackets, did not improve the situation. This was their chance to extort cash from taxi drivers. Loud arguments and shouts of abuse ensued as batons were wielded at windscreens.

We heard the blaring of sirens and Tony tried to steer our Land Rover off the road, but there was no space. A rifle-butt wielded by a uniformed thug thumped on our car roof. Henchmen lent out of the windows of a Peugeot, straining to lash their whips at passers-by. Behind them, the commissioner of police reclined in the back seat of his car like a contented toad. He was travelling to his hometown.

The exhaust of one ramshackle mammy-wagon ahead of our car belched pungent fumes that stung our throats, so we wound up the windows and left Tony to battle with the driving. We sat back and chatted. From our small fortress we could study the bedlam around. It seemed that everyone was in a hurry. The elite heading for the refinery in air-conditioned cars contrasted strongly with the struggling masses. Here was a portrait that depicted the very essence of life in Nigeria. Joy shook her head. 'People in Britain would never believe this.'

At that moment I heard some regular drum-beats and saw in front a procession of Boys' Brigade. They were marching in perfect rhythm, totally oblivious to the surrounding pandemonium. They were young - probably between ten and twelve years old - and clad in navy tailored trousers with knife-edge creases. The golden buttons on their jackets shone and their pillbox hats were tilted at cocky angles. They swung their arms high, much higher than their shoulders. Their strides were long and occasionally they gave a small leap to keep pace with their tall captain who solemnly chanted, 'Left, right, left right.'

As we drove past, Joy and I turned and craned our necks to catch a better glimpse. Their serious expressions showed pride and hope. One very small boy walked in front grasping a staff, held at an oblique angle. He swung it diagonally across his chest with great gusto, exactly to the rhythm of the drumbeats.

This was a precious moment, a time to savour. Joy grabbed my arm and spluttered, 'Did you see them?'

'Yes.' I was lost for words. We both started to laugh though I could have wept for these ordinary people who struggled hard to survive.

Once in Telele, Joy took photographs whilst I resumed searching for water. This time I decided to start near the chief's house, an unlikely place because the ground was raised and rocky. Within minutes, the rods swung together with amazing strength. I could hardly believe it. 'Look at this Joy! There's water right here. It's exactly where the villagers need it. To think I wasted all that time yesterday when it was right here.'

Joy watched the rods swing. Delighted but perhaps doubting such luck, she suggested, 'Maybe water's being stored inside that hut. Wouldn't that cause the rods to respond?'

'Oh dear, I hope not.'

We rushed into the chief's compound, scattering his chickens, and searched around anxiously. His wife allowed us to look inside her house and pointed to three kerosene tins and a large pot that stood near the entrance. To my relief they were dry.

During the days that followed, I visited many villages to locate suitable sites for wells. By evening, storm clouds would gather and the heat was becoming intense ... a sign that the rains would soon come. This would make well construction impossible.

Joy returned to Britain and I became anxious. What had happened to Theo Huitema? One evening a rather battered truck spluttered into the Jacaranda. It was loaded with men and equipment. A sun-tanned Dutchman in his forties climbed out ... Theo Huitema had arrived.

Theo wasted no time in getting started. Refusing my offer of accommodation in town, he preferred to camp in our thatched chalet. His Nigerian workers came from the Jos Plateau area. They slept in the pottery workshop and were happy to eat the local food from Maraba Rido village nearby. I had mustered youths from different villages to join a 'well construction' team. That evening Theo conducted his first engineering class. He spoke fluent Hausa and the youths were very attentive, greatly appreciating his sense of humour. There was laughter and fun, but Theo made everyone work hard. That night we all agreed that he was extremely capable and well organised.

I could hardly keep up with his demands but was determined not to be the cause of any delay. He needed a large quantity of cement, sand, gravel, metal rods, wooden planks and many mechanical items like pulleys and ropes. He used his own equipment but also rigged up some for the young men to use in the future ... he would teach them how construct a reliable well.

A few days later I went to Kakura village and was impressed with the well being dug. The shaft was surprisingly wide and deep. Beside it were rings of reinforced concrete. Theo was pleased to see me. 'We have nearly reached water - if you climb down you'll hear it gushing underground.'

Fearing the walls would cave in I asked, 'Is this safe? Won't the sides collapse?'

Theo looked confident. 'Just as you warned me, the walls are showing signs of crumbling. We're going to lower some rings right now.' I had arrived in time to see the metal tripod and winch used to lower the first ring into the shaft.

Theo worked at other villages, Damisi, Pam Madaki and Telele, supervising the actual digging. Meanwhile he had taught the youths how to mix the cement and mould the reinforced rings.

It was an exciting moment when clean water gushed out at Telele Village - the women danced for joy. Our money was running out, but Sister Rosa rescued our project. She told me that St Columba's Primary School, Durango, Colorado, had raised money for wells. Other individuals from America donated cash in memory of their loved ones - much more valuable than a tombstone. The Rotary club also gave support.

By the time Theo Huitema returned to Jos, he had constructed four excellent wells, all fitted with hand-pumps. The women were overjoyed to see clean water filling their buckets. For me, it was magical because it was a step forward towards better health for the villagers.

***

One morning in August a fierce storm hit the Jacaranda. The wind stripped leaves off the eucalyptus trees and lashed the palm fronds. Awed by the ferocity of the storm, I stood in the doorway of the pottery workshop hesitating about whether or not to dash across the courtyard to the glazing hut. Instead I watched the puddles extending until they merged to form a shallow pond; bougainvillea blossoms dropped into the water and floated like miniature sailing boats. Inside the workshop, rain seeped through the thatched roof and dripped over the bench. Mohammed spread a plastic sheet over the row of storage jars he had thrown that morning.

Just then, two figures appeared, walking through the torrential rain. I soon saw they were the chiefs of Pam Madaki and Telele villages. Drenched, they entered the workshop, their foreheads puckered with frowns. They greeted me politely and without waiting to shake the water from their clothing beckoned to Adam to act as their interpreter. I listened to their hurried speech and recognised a few words like 'mugun zawo' - which means 'bad diarrhoea'.

Adam looked alarmed as he translated. 'They are saying that people in some villages near theirs are dying of diarrhoea. They're afraid that it will reach their people. They are asking for your help.'

Before I could reply, the Chief of Telele knelt down on the hard floor. I felt very uncomfortable to see him kneeling before me. 'Adam, tell him to get up - you know I don't like anyone to kneel - we're all equal.' Adam spoke in Gbagi, gesticulating, but the chief did not move.

I felt unable to communicate with him kneeling like that. 'Tell him that I'll walk away if he doesn't stand up. I don't want anyone to kneel for me.' Flushed with embarrassment, I stepped back as if to leave.

Adam whispered in the chief's ear and took his hand, gently easing him to his feet.

Straining to understand what was being said, I managed to pick out more words. 'Ruwa shinkafa' was repeated several times ... it means 'rice-water'.

'Ma, they say the diarrhoea is very bad, something looking like rice-water pours from the body. Families are dying - husbands, wives and children.' Both chiefs were ringing their hands nervously, lamenting to the pottery staff about the numbers of dead.

I remembered that Eli had once treated a patient suffering from cholera. He had described the ghastly symptoms ... diarrhoea resembling rice water had gushed from the body like a tap. Eli had inserted several drips into the arms and legs of his patient to counteract the dehydration. The chiefs had good reason to frown - their description was very apt.

It was a Saturday and government offices were closed for the weekend. At this stage I could only give advice. 'You must keep away from those villages. Don't go near them.' The chiefs listened intently as I continued. 'You'll need to hold a meeting. Make sure everyone hears what you say because this could save their lives.'

I was aware of the lack of any sanitation in those villages where people relieved themselves in the bushes. The stream that flowed near Telele and Pam Madaki villages would doubtless carry the disease from those upstream. Adam continued to translate my advice. 'Don't drink any water from your stream. Keep well away from it. You have new wells so make sure you use them. Boil your drinking water.' I also warned them to keep flies off food and wash hands. They listened earnestly as the rain outside softened. I liked these chiefs who always struggled to help their impoverished people. As they left the workshop, I felt determined to buy some cholera vaccine but did not wish to raise their hopes in case it was unavailable. They had expected me to give them some magic medicine and seemed reluctant to leave. I supplied them sachets of rehydration salts and promised to visit their village the next morning, for it was a Sunday and the entire population would be gathered in church.

On my way home I called on Nurse Isa who kept a small provision shop in town; I told him about the cholera outbreak. He looked very concerned. 'We must buy some vaccine. Unfortunately there are many different strains of cholera - we won't know which strain we're dealing with, but still, it's worth trying.' Together we drove around town, searching for the vaccine until at last we found some in a pharmacy in the most congested part of town. The owner seemed a decent person; many drugs are faked in Nigeria; vaccines have to be checked carefully in case they are out of date. I had no cash so we agreed to return the next morning. We would need to use our cold box - we also ordered dozens of disposable syringes.

The next day I left home in brilliant sunshine - the sky was cloudless. Blue sky in August comes with intense heat and I knew a thunderstorm would follow later. We hoped we would have finished work in Telele long before any rain. Halfway there, the heat became more oppressive, and dense white cumulo-nimbus clouds built up in the sky. It was eleven in the morning when we reached the muddy track that led to the villages. Progress was slow as bushes had invaded our route and Tony had to lop off a few branches. It seemed no vehicle had passed that way for weeks. All the time we could hear the rumbling of thunder as the sky darkened. When the track descended into a valley, thick mud covered our wheel hubs and Tony pulled the lever to use four-wheel drive. We heard deafening claps of thunder as streaks of lightning hit the granite hills nearby. It was too late to retreat - it started to pour with rain but we were almost there, so we pressed on. We saw the stream and parked the Land Rover on higher ground. The plank bridge was visible, inches above the rushing water. We unloaded our syringes and cold-box and walked gingerly towards the stream. Soaked and with rain dripping down my back, I dreaded balancing along the narrow planks ... they would be slippery.

We were startled when five men emerged from behind a tree. They wore black rain-cloaks with hoods and I knew that we were vulnerable in such an isolated spot so I was relieved to see they were young men we had trained as health workers. They greeted us with genuine delight and took the luggage, insisting on carrying even my small handbag. They led us to the bridge where two of them took my hands, one in front and the other behind and guided me over the cascading torrents. I didn't complain but my bifocals were steamed up and the slippery planks, held together with bicycle chains, moved as we crossed.

We trooped along the winding pathway to the village completely drenched - there was no point in hurrying from the downpour. At that moment I heard children's soprano voices rising above the thunder; I paused to make sure it was real. The old church was packed with village people singing a beautiful hymn. I heard the words 'Alleluya, alleluya', shrill happy voices. As the hymn ended we walked into the church where hundreds of smiling people clapped, their faces radiant.

The chief came forward and shaking our hands led us to the front, where we were given seats facing the congregation. He was beaming when he asked me to pray. For once I was stuck for words and turned to Isa. 'You do it. They won't understand my English.' Isa rose to his feet and prayed as devoutly as a parson. He took ages and I began to shiver in my sodden clothes.

After the service, the people lined up for their vaccinations. The gentle chief organised the line and held each child, calmly soothing some infants who cried in fear. Women came next, followed by men. Once the chief was sure that everyone had been injected, he took his.

We drove home, along that slippery track, stopping briefly at Pam Madaki to vaccinate more people. Their chief was equally delighted to see us. They had been waiting all morning. I still felt anxious, unsure that our vaccine would work.

On the way home, my anxiety changed to relief and I forgot about the mud and the slippery road. Tony, Isa and I savoured the magical experience we had shared together ... we were drunk with happiness.

As the planting season ended and the rains subsided I returned to Telele. My beautiful people had not caught cholera.

***

In those early days of roving clinics something happened that changed the direction of the project. It was during a roving clinic held in Damisi that a girl of about four was brought to us. Her feet had been severely burnt and her toes were missing. The child could neither stand nor walk on the inflamed stumps that now represented her feet. Horrified, I listened as nurse Hajiya questioned the mother.

'Sanu mamma, how did this happen?'

The mother looked down to avoid eye contact and mumbled, 'She walked into a fire.'

Hajiya scowled at the woman. 'Haba. Oh no. She must have stood in that fire for some time to have her toes burnt off. Were you there?'

The mother looked perplexed and her eyes wandered as if she was searching the sky for an answer.

Hajiya handled one of the stumps and frowned. 'Why didn't you come earlier? This must have happened several months ago.'

The woman had by now assumed a vacant expression but Hajiya would not be deterred. 'Was it before the harvest?

'Yi - yes.

Normally Hajiya was gentle with patients but when she turned to me I could see that she was furious. 'Ma, this child was burnt at least six months ago. God knows the agony she was put through. This mother knows very well what happened; she's afraid to speak the truth. She was probably too ashamed

155

to bring the girl to us earlier.'

I stared at the remnants of feet, trying to fathom how this little child would ever manage to walk. She wore a pretty wrapper or cloth, tied around her waist but her expression was forlorn. It seemed that her normal childlike sparkle had been snuffed out.

Hajiya's outburst had startled me - she was usually a good-natured person. I felt puzzled. 'What exactly are you implying?'

'This child has been deliberately burnt. My guess is that she had a convulsion. People in these parts are very superstitious and believe fits are due to witchcraft. They drive evil spirits away by burning. I've seen cases like this before.'

I shuddered at the thought of this small girl being deliberately burnt. The mother, a pathetic-looking woman, gently stroked the child's plaited hair and begged Hajiya to make her walk again. There was nothing we could do.

A few weeks later, another girl was brought to Jacaranda. One of her arms was scorched to the bone. The remaining muscles had shrunk, contorting her tiny fingers. The old man who carried her was her grandfather who said he had walked for two days from some distant hills. He obviously adored the child. Our wonderful surgeon agreed to operate and graft skin to disguise the scars; the shrivelled hand would always be deformed.

There were other cases. Children were occasionally brought to our clinic with agonising abscesses caused by dirty injections. Isa told me that the local medicine man had most likely injected a harmful potion into the buttocks. In those parts, it was believed that cows urine was a powerful remedy for certain illnesses.

Another day, a chubby baby boy, paper white with anaemia and bleeding badly, was brought to us. His chest was striated with deep cuts, inflicted to rid him of fever. He was another victim of the so-called 'doctor' in Maraba Rido.

After a particularly sad day in Damisi, I talked to Eli about the appalling ignorance and superstition. 'How can people cause so much pain to a helpless child?'

Eli looked concerned and spoke with feeling. 'You could report that quack to the local government but he'd become your enemy. The real remedy is to educate the parents. Better education and enlightenment would rid the people of their ignorance and superstitions.'

I knew Eli was right. Damisi and Kakura had no schools. Apart from the pastor and the Moslem cleric, the people were illiterate.

That evening we were invited to a reception at the British High Commission to celebrate the Queen's birthday. Drinks were flowing and people were munching fried chicken, large shrimps and canapés. Guests filled the lounge and overflowed onto a terrace. After my day in Damisi, this was a different world. Well-nourished civil servants, diplomats and business executives raised their voices above the tuneless band, scrumming at the bar to recharge their glasses and reaching out to fill their mouths with tasty morsels delivered on silver platters. In spite of the heat, the expatriate men wore lounge suits; their wives displayed their most fancy cocktail dresses. Nigerian men were dressed traditionally in crisp Swiss lace and brocade - the women wore their largest head-ties of stiff shiny cloth threaded with gold yarn that blended with costly gold jewellery. The smell of human perfumes mingled with the scent of the colourful frangipani blossoms that had been floodlit for this auspicious occasion.

Suddenly the police band struck up the well-rehearsed Nigerian National Anthem and everyone stood to attention. A rather shaky 'God Save the Queen' followed - the trumpeter struggling to reach the high notes. Relieved after this brief ceremony, the mood lightened and official guests started to leave. The expatriate men removed their jackets and got down to more drinking. I noticed the Deputy High Commissioner making his way towards Eli and me. He shook hands warmly and fixed his eyes on me. 'Are you still spending your time out in the villages? How's it all going? Are you still helping those Jacaranda Children?'

I yearned to describe the poverty, but this was not the right place. Relating the plight of the village people would most likely 'kill' the evening. Cautiously I replied 'I need to build a school - I'm looking for help.'

The High Commissioner replied briskly, 'You're in luck tonight. Over there is the man you need to speak to, he's a senior person in Nomadic Education. I'll introduce you.'

He led Eli and me over to a group of Nigerians and introduced us to a young man, dressed in blue damask, his head topped with a brightly embroidered fez. Handsome and well spoken, he seemed genuinely interested to hear about the children of Damisi. I waited eagerly for his reaction.

'You are the type of person we need. You have described exactly what Nomadic Education is looking for. Would you come to my office tomorrow at ten and we will discuss the matter further? I feel sure we can build your school.' His gentle words were like music in my ears.

I did not sleep well after the Queen's Birthday party. The hum of our air conditioner would usually drown the sounds of the night but once again there was no electricity. Bathed in sweat I cursed the persistent mosquito that pinged in my ear and the over-exuberant cricket with its high-pitched squeak. The deafening croaks of courting frogs in the pond below our window were the last straw. Restless, I went downstairs to wait for sunrise.

My visit to Nomadic Education did not go as planned. The handsome young man had apparently been called away to a meeting. After wasting my morning, waiting for him, I was flippantly told to come back the next day. Determined to have a school for Damisi, I persevered for days and then weeks, but my appointments were usually cancelled without apology. I pandered to their request for architectural plans and a quantity surveyor's report. I would stomach humiliation if it would result in a school for Damisi. Exasperated, one morning I cornered a senior member of Nomadic Education who at last put me out of my agony: 'Your application has not been accepted - there are not enough nomads in Damisi.' Sick with disappointment, I turned away wondering why they had raised my hopes for so long. I knew there were many Fulani children in the Damisi area who were without any decent education.

Whispers of my disappointment must have reached the British High Commissioner, because his secretary telephoned and asked me to submit a proposal to their office. I worked long into the night to put down the relevant information. Within a few days a cheque arrived, enough to build the first classroom.

My budget was tight because I had forgotten to include desks and a blackboard on the proposal. I therefore decided to call a meeting in Damisi and insisted that women should be present. Almost the entire village attended but the women sat apart from the men and seemed too submissive to speak. As expected, the chief, who lived apart from his people did not show up but other Fulani and Gbagi elders made helpful suggestions.

One old Fulani man with a long white beard offered a suitable plot of land. The Gbagis, not to be outdone, volunteered to start making mud blocks. The women agreed to carry water for mixing the mud. The feeling of enthusiasm and unity was wonderful as folk chattered in excitement. Later Danlami and Adam told me that it was unusual for Fulani and Gbagi to mix in this way - it had never happened before.

The next morning Tony used our farm tractor and dragged an old water tank to the school site. A local builder started digging the foundations whilst the men moulded hundreds of blocks that were piled in the sun to dry. The builder taught the people how to lay blocks, using a spirit level to ensure the walls were straight.

I purchased some solid metal shutters as windows. These were arranged to give cross ventilation. The roof was made of best quality zinc and the timbers were well seasoned. There was not enough money for a ceiling.

The most expensive item was cement. This was used for the floor and for plastering the walls. Eli donated cream and green paint. In the evenings the local people gathered under the shady porch and proudly admired their school. There was just enough money to pay for the desks and blackboard, already ordered from a local carpenter.

The day the new school opened was exciting for everybody. An interesting mixture of children came. Their ages ranged from small infants to spotty youths. There were equal numbers of Fulani and Gbagi - many small girls carried tiny babies on their backs. Over forty children were registered.

Later in the morning a delegation of elders came to express their thanks. They also told me that they had heard Nomadic Education broadcasting the opening of *their* new school over the radio. How we all laughed, but the Fulani elders were disgusted.

I named the school Amamus Damisi from the Latin 'We love Damisi'. Within a few weeks the Australian Embassy provided a cheque for a second classroom and with more generous donations, the school gradually expanded to a full Primary School with six classrooms. Amamus schools were eventually built in Telele, Pam Madaki and Kakura.

One evening the old Fulani man who had donated the land beckoned to me. He looked contented though he was growing old and his eyes seemed dim. We stood together for a few moments as he leant on a stick and pointed to the distant flame burning at the Oil Refinery. His son translated what he wanted to say to me: 'Now that my grandchildren have a school and are able to learn, I pray that one day they will work in that place where I see the flame.'

Looking into his kind, wrinkled face I replied, 'Allah ya sa - May Allah grant your wish.'

What counts is not the enormity of the task, but the size of the courage.
Matthieu Ricard

CAPITAL KADUNA
May 1992

I left the Jacaranda early in the afternoon. I wanted to avoid the usual traffic hold-up in Sabon Tasha as my car was loaded with freshly- plucked chickens and ripe mangoes.

I reached our house by about four and noticed Eli's car was missing from the carport. Sariki, a handsome Tuareg from Niger, was on guard duty. He pointed to the space, laughing and gesticulating with his arms, clearly imitating a golf swing. I had no need to guess where Eli was.

The house seemed quiet and I went upstairs to bathe and change out of my khaki trousers and shirt. Once in the bedroom I turned on the television. *The High Chaparral* had just started. Our bathroom adjoined the bedroom and I relaxed in the warm bubbles, dreaming. From the bath I could just see the screen, an exciting scene with galloping horses, stampeding cattle and gunfire.

After a while, the bangs became very loud - the noise was not part of the film. I leapt out of the bath and peered through the window. There was black smoke and I could hear shouting. At that moment Eli drove his ancient Mercedes through the open gates. What a relief to see him! He came upstairs to the bedroom looking grave. 'Those people out there are quite mad. They're burning cars and killing people.'

'Killing? Surely not? Why?'

'Come and see. You'll have a shock.' He led me to the far end of our house, to the children's wing, where a window overlooked the crossroads. Beyond was a petrol station. To my horror a mob was attacking passers-by, striking them with cudgels. I stared in disbelief when petrol was doused over one man who was then set alight.

Ogbaje tapped on the door and came in looking worried. 'Master, have you seen what's going on in the road?'

'Yes, I had a lucky escape. The mob was about to set on me when some older men ordered them off. The ambulance from Gwandu Clinic was on fire - the driver stood no chance.'

Sickened by his words, my fear increased. I could hear raised voices coming from our sitting room and rushed downstairs. Many women and children had fled to our house. There was pandemonium making it almost impossible to hear the loudspeaker blaring from the nearby Mosque. I rushed to the outside courtyard and picked out the word 'jihad' but the bangs and crashes and blood curdling whoops of the mob drowned all other words.

One lady, a stranger to me, wailed in a high-pitched voice, 'They killed my husband. I escaped over your wall … I had to leave him alone to die.' The baby on her back was sleeping.

Ogbaje's wife and daughters came from the kitchen, terror in their eyes. Our male workers were gathered outside the backdoor - gardeners, guards and drivers. Eli ushered them to the front of the house, where a panic-stricken woman struggled to hoist her children over our wall. Our drivers rushed to help her. Eli spoke with authority. 'We must try to keep that mob out. If they get in, we'll have to fight.' I noticed Zuru the gardener had already armed himself with a locally made hoe. I grabbed Eli's brand new Ping golf clubs and handed one iron to each man. They were the best weapons I could find. When Eli did not object, I knew the situation was serious.

As the light faded we listened to the sickening thuds of cars being battered, their occupants tortured to death. There was no electricity that night and we were afraid that starting our noisy generator would only draw attention to our house.

Hot and fearful I sat on the floor, trying to shut out the agonising screams.

There were about thirty people in our sitting room. We could do no more than wait. To pass the time I decided to organise Ogbaje's daughters and some young wives to cook a chicken pepper stew. Before long they were cutting up the chickens and frying onions and tomatoes. The task distracted them but I doubted whether anyone would be able to face food.

The phone rang. It was Eli's sister who lived close-by. He seemed startled by her words. I dreaded bad news and shook his arm. 'Tell me what's happened.'

Eli's voice was quiet. 'Dennis was at a meeting. On his way home, he met the mob at these crossroads. They threw a huge rock through his windscreen and it sounds as if he's got a broken jaw.'

'Thank God he's alive. How did he manage to get home?'

'One of his junior workers was amongst the mob. That's why they let him go.'

Later, the phone rang again. I picked up the receiver, anticipating more trouble. It was from someone working for the British High Commission. I strained to hear the muffled voice.

'Are you OK? Good. We're coming to rescue you. You're in a danger zone. Hold on … we're close to your house.'

Did this person really know what was happening around our house? I warned him, 'It's not safe. Stay away - the mob will attack you.'

His reply was firm. 'We're well equipped to handle riots. At any moment you'll see our headlights. Get ready to open your gate.'

Sure enough we saw bright lights approaching and a brand-new Land Rover drove in, its diplomatic number plates lit-up. Two men jumped out. 'Are you ready to go? Hurry. Jump in.'

Eli and I looked at each other. We did not speak. Ogbaje touched my arm. 'Madam, you're not going to leave us?'

'No Ogbaje, we won't do that.'

The rioters in the street, attracted by our voices and headlights, started baying like bloodhounds. There was smoke in the air. Eli turned to the two men. 'We can't abandon all these people sheltering in our house. They'll panic.'

The diplomats looked rather put out. Shrugging in disbelief they handed Eli a short-wave radio set and pointed to the button. 'Press that if you need to communicate.' Hurriedly they jumped back into the Land Rover. 'Keep in touch every hour. Let us know of any changes. You've missed your chance - we won't come back again.'

I was left with a ghastly sinking feeling. An hour or so later a gigantic petrol tanker appeared and parked right across our gates, barring any hope of escape. I felt terrible claustrophobia and voiced my fears to Eli. 'Do you think there's fuel in that tanker? If it blows up, our house will go with it.'

Eli already looked worried. 'I don't know why it's there. I suspect they're siphoning petrol from it.'

The next morning the tanker started its engine and roared away into the village just before army lorries approached. I peeped over the wall and saw several bodies lying on the tarmac. I saw the burnt ambulance and was thankful for

Eli's survival. Later that morning a dark green refuse lorry appeared. Some men, muffled to keep the stench from their nostrils, were collecting bodies. They heaved them over the sides of the lorry and drove away.

The rioting continued for two more days. Badly shaken, Eli and I later heard about the extent of the destruction. Hundreds of people had been slaughtered throughout Kaduna State and over a hundred churches had been torched. There was a terrible stench when I passed the hospital three days later. The refuse lorries were unloading decomposing bodies - the mortuary was full. The trouble had started over some longstanding land disputes in an outlying town called Zango Kataf where the government had unfairly handled an already-tense situation. Clashes had arisen between the indigenous Christian Katafs and the Moslem Hausas. The situation had escalated. Some of the seriously wounded and dead Hausas were carried to hospital in Kaduna. This news was not well received by the Hausas who wanted revenge. They announced from their Mosques that Christians had killed Moslems in Zango Kataf and urged all true believers to come out for a jihad.

I felt nervous about our future, living in that Ungwan Rimi area of Kaduna. I would never again feel relaxed in our house. Nothing would be the same. 'Now I understand how the Jews must have felt before the Holocaust,' I told Eli. 'The fortunate ones got out of Germany in time. Living here, surrounded by Mosques, we're sitting ducks. We had a lucky escape but I believe it's a warning. We must move away from this area.'

Eli strongly disagreed. 'I'm going to increase the height of our wall and fortify the house. I'll make sure it's safe for you.

This is our home, my lifetime's work. I won't be driven away by anyone. We were here first. Think of the years we've lived in this house - don't you remember when this area was all farmland? I can't imagine driving home from the clinic to any other place. This is our home.'

The quality of life in Nigeria had in many ways deteriorated since 1962, the year when our ship had docked in Apapa. At that time Kaduna was known as the Garden City of Nigeria because there were magnificent flowerbeds with orange canna lilies planted on the roundabouts. Kaduna was clean in those days; avenues of trees lined the roads. Now the town was more like a rubbish dump. Litter was heaped everywhere and pigs wandered in the overpopulated suburbs, wallowing in the filthy open gutters. Black plastic bags, locally known as *ledders,* floated about and some caught on branches of the few surviving trees. What had become of the vultures that once perched in mahogany trees overlooking the railway station?

The pyramids of groundnuts and acres of cotton fields we used to pass on the road to Kano had disappeared and the huge textile factories in Kaduna were closing down. Other small businesses had been forced into bankruptcy. The local currency, the naira, once worth sixty-eight pence, was now valued at less than a penny. Prices in the market had risen and people couldn't afford to buy a pair of shoes.

There was little hope of employment for school leavers or graduates; this created 'an army of hungry, angry, restless youths'. Violent robberies by organised gangs had become commonplace and it was too risky for anyone to venture along the highways after dark. The cancer of corruption was spreading. It was commonly believed, that to exist one had to bribe and cheat. Nigeria was likened to 'the spoilt child that had been provided with everything possible but had grown up to become a delinquent.'

Why had Nigeria fallen so low? Oil? … the 'excrement of the devil'.

***

The roving clinic had been exceptionally busy one morning in April. As the sun went low in the sky, mothers with screaming infants congregated under a mango tree, waiting for attention. Flies, attracted by human smells, came to feast on snot and sweat. This day tension had been building up like a storm, as the endless tail of patients seemed to expand. Nurse Charity, a recently recruited Yoruba nurse, did not improve the situation. She had previously worked in General Hospitals and was unfamiliar with shy Gbagi and Fulani women. Slightly overweight, she suffered in the heat, and was inclined to snap at patients.

We had been working since early morning and were wilting with thirst and tiredness. Over a hundred patients had been registered that day. Our other nurse had taken some serious cases to the doctor in town, leaving just three of us to cope. As we were preparing to finish, a village chief appeared; he guided a dejected looking woman towards Charity saying, 'Go on. Speak.' But the woman hung her head in silence.

The chief was unusually ruffled. 'Speak. You'll have to tell her.' The woman moved forward and whispered something inaudible.

The nurse's eyes were glaring. 'Speak up. How am I meant to hear you?'

The woman shrunk back, coyly looking at her feet,

169

then whispered, 'I get belly.'

Charity looked at the woman's card and read her name aloud. 'Ruth.' She also saw the word *Caesarean,* written in red, and threw her arms into the air, bellowing like a wounded animal. 'You have had one Caesarean already. You were warned not to have any more babies. Who will pay this time? Are you are the wife of a rich man - someone who can afford to go to the big hospital? Why didn't you attend the family planning clinic?'

Esther and I had been updating records and dispensing medicines. We knew Ruth well; she was a reliable woman who regularly attended health workshops. Charity's aggressive behaviour would have to be curtailed. I moved forward and tapped her shoulder. 'Take it easy, Charity. Try to be gentle, you can see the patient's already distressed.'

As Ruth turned away to hide her misery she whispered, 'My husband didn't allow me to attend family planning.'

Charity more subdued, lowered her tone. 'Why not?'

A stir and almost a giggle came from a group of women who had been straining to eavesdrop. The mother hesitated for a moment and then spoke. 'He believes your medicine will reduce his manhood.'

Charity reacted like an erupting volcano. 'Where's your husband?'

'Me? I'm here.' A ragged man came forward, knotting the string that held up his trousers.

Charity fired her questions. 'What's wrong with you? Are you trying to kill your wife? How many pikins do you have?'

A crowd of snotty nosed children with pendulous bellies was observing the scene, their eyes growing larger. They gazed admiringly at their father who had two wives. He started counting on his fingers then squared himself up to the irate nurse and proudly declared, 'Nine.'

His bold answer raised a huge cheer from the crowd and all tension evaporated.

On our homeward journey we discussed Ruth's problem. Her medical record showed that she had a small pelvis - undoubtedly she would need a Caesarean. Such an operation would be costly. Our funds were very low - the donors were specific about how their funding should be used and there was no provision for private medical bills. Esther made a clicking sound in the back of her throat, a sound of sympathy, then murmured, 'Allah kawo - May God provide.'

During the weeks that followed, Ruth hung around during our roving clinics, looking increasingly worried as her pregnancy advanced. I advised her to come into town when her labour started though at that time I did not know how I would cope.

One morning, a few weeks later, I stopped at the Lafiya Clinic and met a crowd of people gathered. I recognised Ruth with her husband; the chief was also there with a crowd of older women. I guessed Ruth was in labour. Our doctor examined her and reiterated that she would need a Caesarean.

Eli was away in Bida. I groped in my handbag and brought out all my money, five-hundred naira - at that time the equivalent of thirty pounds. I handed it to the chief. 'I'm afraid this is all I have. You'd better take Ruth to the Mission Hospital - the one she attended last time would be best - maybe the doctor there will understand how poor she is.' I felt bothered over my meagre contribution.

Later that morning, I went to the hospital to find that Ruth had still not been admitted. Humphrey rushed forward, relieved to see me. 'The doctor told us to bring twenty thousand naira - we begged him to reduce the bill. After a great deal of persuasion, he reduced it to ten thousand. He has refused to admit Ruth until we pay.'

I felt relieved about the bill. 'Ten thousand is reasonable but these villagers are bound to think it's too much. To them it's a fortune. Where's the chief?'

'He went back to his village for help. He said he'd ask his friends to contribute.'

The village was miles away and transport was difficult. The chief would have to walk several miles. I decided to go home to search for more cash. Later, I went back to the hospital and was pleased that the chief had returned. We sat under a tree, endeavouring to sort out a pile of musty banknotes. Humphrey counted them looking pleased when I added an extra three thousand naira. 'It's enough. We've made it.' He bundled the money into a plastic bag and went to pay.

Soon Ruth was admitted to the ward and prepared for her operation. Between contractions, the nurse helped her onto a trolley and wheeled her towards the operating theatre; one midwife whispered that there was foetal distress. An older woman tried to comfort Ruth. The theatre was occupied so her trolley was parked in the corridor. It seemed that time was running out. To ease my anxiety, I strolled outside.

The pastor had arrived with many more villagers. He summoned his flock to a shady corner where they formed a circle and started praying. After a while, the shrill sound of women ululating interrupted the mediations. The villagers stopped praying, hesitated for a moment and then stampeded towards the hospital, leaving their pastor standing alone, most bewildered.

They found Ruth, on the trolley, nursing a beautiful baby boy. His birth had been completely natural; he had been born unexpectedly in that corridor outside the theatre.

There was tremendous excitement coupled with relief. The ecstatic father behaved as if this had been his first child. Humphrey, overwhelmed with excitement came over to me, wiping his eyes. 'Ma, they want you to choose a name.'

I paused and then, in a flash had an idea. 'What's the word for a miracle?'

Humphrey gazed at the sky, racking his brain and then said, 'Abun mamaki.'

I whispered the words and loved the sound … they seemed perfect. Looking enquiringly at the happy mother I whispered, 'Abun Mamaki? Would you call him Abun Mamaki?' She smiled and all became still. Perhaps we had witnessed a real miracle.

When I told our doctor at the Lafiya Clinic about the natural birth of Abun Mamaki she shared my joy, clapping and smiling. 'The disproportion was marked - moreover that baby had a very large head. I find it hard to believe that Ruth delivered her baby naturally. It certainly was a miracle.'

***

By October the rainy season dies away but the last storms are always violent. They build up during the intense afternoon heat and erupt during the night when winds lash across the savannah plains followed by thunder and streak lightning. During these storms, roofs are ripped off the village houses and crops are usually damaged.

The rains end abruptly and the next seven months are

completely dry. The harmattan wind usually appears in November, wafting from the Sahara desert and bearing a red dusty veil. It cools the heated earth and restores energy to village people still exhausted from farming. As the humidity decreases, there are fewer mosquitoes and therefore less malaria.

When the harmattan blows Fulani cattle gallop and leap as if they are enjoying the beautiful air. At night the village people dance and drum under starlit skies. Fulani youths joust with long sticks practising for a ceremony called 'shoro.' This is their chance to prove their manhood and show that they are brave.

During a shoro initiation, the Fulani people gather wearing their most colourful clothes. Tall, fine-featured women adorn themselves with colourful jewellery and paint their faces with locally made mascara, rouge and lipstick. Their short embroidered bodices reveal slender waists that gyrate to tantalise the youths. The married women display their agate beads, greatly valued as part of their dowry. Fulani men wear colourful trapeze shaped shirts and tight breeches, all finely embroidered.

When shoro takes place, the youths whip their rivals on their rib cages using long sticks. To be initiated into manhood means they have to endure this beating without flinching. To achieve an emotionless expression they hold small hand mirrors and stare at their reflections.

The beatings leave the youths badly bruised with weals across their chests. So brutal is this ceremony that occasionally one will end up in the general hospital with broken ribs. The newly initiated men happily choose their bride but still have to pay a dowry before they are free to marry.

It was a beautiful morning at the time of the shoro

initiations when I was decorating pots at the Jacaranda, struggling to keep up with the potters who were having an unusual burst of energy. Large decanters and storage jars were rapidly accumulating on my table. I felt determined to keep up, fully aware that we needed pots for an exhibition that was fast approaching. Our customers always wanted African designs and I was the only designer. There were never enough hours in the day to fulfil these orders. I started working on a huge vase, creating a village scene with huts, baobab trees and elephants when Esther came from the shop.

'Ma, some people from Panja are here. They want to see you.' I groaned.

'You attend to them, I'm busy.'

Esther frowned. 'They have a problem and they've come far, Ma, please see them.' I continued to work on an elephant but its back legs were already askew, so I threw my brush into the iron oxide and followed her into the shop.

Three men were waiting there; they were weather-beaten and covered in harmattan dust that made their hair and eyebrows appear white. I assumed they had travelled on the back of a lorry because their clothing looked dusty. Their faces were dry like lizard's skin and their eyes were watery. Esther translated.

'We have come from Panja. Our chief sent us to seek your help. The children in Panja are dying and he wants you to come to our village.'

Panja was miles away, far off the main road and our project was financially overstretched. The little funding we had from Cafod was almost finished. I knew that by starting primary health care in many villages, I had overspent. 'Esther, try to explain to them that we can't take on any more work. We haven't got enough nurses and we've used up our money. Besides, Panja is miles from here.'

The men listened but continued to urge me. I became curious to find out why their children were dying.

'What happens when your children are ill? What do they complain of?'

'Cough, a cough that kills. Our smallest babies are the first to die.'

'Have your children ever been immunised?'

The men shook their heads. 'The government health centre is miles away, too far for us to walk.'

'Have you reported this illness at the local government health centre?'

'Yes, but they won't come. They say they have no vehicle.'

The men listened sympathetically as I explained about our worn out vehicles and our lack of money. They were gentle people and when eventually they turned to leave, one spoke.

'If you can't come to help us, would you at least come to see the graves of our children?'

The next day long before sunrise we were on the road, heading for Panja. It took us four hours to reach the village. Our journey along the main road wound through hills ... the same blue hills that were visible in the distance from the Jacaranda.

Leaving the main road we drove through rich farmland along an endless track. We passed many small hamlets and noticed an exceptionally large number of children crawling along the ground, crippled from polio. The track ended at a clearing in front of a church. All was quiet but gradually the village people appeared. Before long parents and children surrounded us. Soon there was little space to unload our supplies.

We immediately knew that the killer disease was whooping cough. The children were having fits of uncontrollable coughing and whooping and I noticed some tiny babies were gasping for breath, eyes bloodshot.

We unloaded boxes of erythromycin, cough syrups and vitamins, realising that supplies would run out. Our nurses Mercy, Hajiya and Isa divided the children into lines according to their ages and set to work. I recorded names and counted tablets. I became puzzled that mothers were lifting their children into my arms, one by one and wondered why? Looking at their tiny faces, I felt their hot foreheads and held their hands as the afternoon sun sunk red in the sky and as the queues continued.

Over two hundred cases had been recorded when I had to stand up to stretch my aching back. An agitated mother grabbed my arm tugging firmly and speaking in a language I could not understand. Hajiya explained.

'She says you haven't even touched her child.'

'What does she mean? I have recorded his name.'

'Yes, but she wants you to lay your hand on her child.'

Rather surprised, I protested.

'I'm not a healer. I'm not into that kind of thing.'

Hajiya replied, 'They believe in you. Don't disappoint them. It comforts the mothers.'

I now understood why they had been placing the children on my lap. What had I been doing? Playing God? My cheeks were burning with shame as Hajiya spoke.

'Didn't you realise that they believe you're a healer?'

Distressed mothers waited and I paused to give the matter some thought. Then I took a deep breath and one by one took each child onto my knee, feeling their burning foreheads and whispering, 'God bless you.'

After visiting Panja I went to visit my friend Sister Rosa. She had guided me since the early days of our project. She knew I was not religious and never forced the issue. She was full of wisdom about primary health care and it was through her guidance that we had been granted funding from Cafod.

At first I spoke about our water project because Sister Rosa had introduced me to Theo, the well engineer. Eventually I came to the point, feeling rather ashamed. 'The village people seem to think I'm some kind of a healer. I don't know what to do about this and feel a terrible fraud. The question is should I continue? I don't want to deceive them.'

Sister Rosa looked at me thoughtfully for a few moments and then replied, 'If you are able to reassure the mothers in this way, I see no harm in it. A relaxed mother will help her child better than a frightened, tense mother. Touching is healing.' I breathed a sigh of relief and departed.

***

In the early nineties, it became necessary to register our project with the Kaduna State government. I approached some responsible friends, mainly doctors, to act as trustees. The project was named Hope for the Village Child. This was a step forward because it meant that we could apply to larger organisations like Unicef for funding. The dictator, General Babangida, was the head of state and had been in command since 1985. We were struggling to run the clinics as we were very short of cash for medical supplies.

Petrol scarcity became one of the worst problems.

Queues, several miles long and especially thick around filling stations, caused traffic chaos everywhere. To fuel our thirsty Land Rover was a nightmare. Tony would sleep at the filling station, sometimes for two to three nights, often to be sold just half a tank. Desperate to reach the clinics, I was compelled to buy black market petrol. Youths dealing in this illegal trade operated in the streets around our house and whenever police vehicles approached, they concealed their funnels and jerry cans beneath our culvert. Transport costs soared and inflation bit harder.

Maryam Babangida launched her controversial program called Better Life for Rural Women, more commonly known as Better Life for Rich Women. Glamorous and self confident, she took the nation by storm. She dressed flamboyantly, and became known as the 'First Lady', imitating the American presidential system. She mobilised many military wives and rapidly gained power, especially in the health sector. Massive resources were made available to her. In 1992, the Central Bank reported that the Better Life Program had cost the nation 400 million naira. This did not include salaries, vehicles and other overheads. She frivolously organised elaborate Better Life headquarters in state capitals. The multi-million building constructed in Abuja offered lavish accommodation for her 'ruling women' and included a Hall of Fame to honour distinguished Nigerian women; portraits of wives of the military junta were prominently displayed amongst great women back in history. Her achievements were applauded with honorary doctorates and chieftaincy titles. In 1991 she was awarded the prestigious Hunger Prize. General Babangida set up a National Women's Commission in tribute to his wife's programme. Due to rivalry between the wives of military governors and the civil servants, Better Life and the Women's Commission coexisted uncomfortably. The climax of this jealousy resulted in the Commission's Chairperson, Professor Awe, an internationally renowned historian, being ruthlessly locked up.

Normally, vaccines were supplied to Hope for the Village Child by the local government. The person there in charge of Primary Health despaired over his meagre allocation and pointed to many empty fridges ... he explained that he was still awaiting supplies. Whilst Humphrey, my assistant, stood by the car, a nurse whispered to him that one chemist near the main market had ample stock of vaccines. Wasting no time, we went straight there. Sure enough, there were vaccines galore - anyone could buy them but the price was outrageous. I studied the labels on the vials and was sickened to note that they were identical to those supplied by government. I was later advised that if I needed supplies, I should register at the Better Life Headquarters in Kaduna. Many Nigerians were dismayed when the Queen invited General Babangida, a military dictator, with his family to dine at Buckingham Palace.

In 1993 General Abacha became the new Commander in Chief of the Armed Forces and President of Nigeria. He was more ruthless than Babangida and anyone who got in his way did so at their peril. He awarded huge contracts to his family and friends and transferred billions into foreign bank accounts. His wife, Mariam, started Family Support in place of her predecessor's Better Life. Vaccines became scarcer than ever. Meanwhile as inflation soared, the value of the naira fell. Essential commodities became scarce and electricity and water supplies frequently failed due to the lack of spare parts. The Nigerian Electric Power Authority was better known as 'no electric power at all'. Anyone experiencing faults on their lines had to pay a heavy goro (kola-nut or bribe) before the engineers would help. Badly maintained vehicles broke down on the pot-holed roads and many were abandoned … it seemed that everything was falling apart in Nigeria.

One afternoon I noticed my potters looking miserable. 'What's wrong? You all look worried.'

'Ma, there's no fertiliser this year. We've paid our deposits to the local government but still the fertiliser hasn't come.'

Bawa, who had many children, added, 'If we don't have fertiliser our harvest will fail - our families will starve.'

Adam pointed to the road. 'Look there's another one. We keep seeing trailers loaded with fertiliser going past. They're for rich people. That farm opposite had three trailer loads delivered yesterday.'

Philip spoke angrily. 'How can one man use so much? We just need two or three bags … it's unfair.' I listened and realised that his problem would affect thousands of farmers in rural Nigeria.

Several weeks later some damp-looking bags of fertiliser were on sale in the market. The price was exorbitant and in any case it had come too late. The guinea corn and maize plants were already stunted.

Perhaps it was due to poverty that armed robberies became widespread in Nigeria but this did not explain the violence used. Eli and I had many restless nights when our Rottweilers barked fiercely, and outside was pitch black due to NEPA failure. Robbers would usually strike in the early hours of the morning, sometimes taking over several houses with military precision. Victims were beaten up and sometimes murdered. One missionary lost his eye when he resisted the marauders who raped his young wife. Eli travelled to Bida frequently - an added stress. I dreaded that he would be attacked on the road. He assured me that his twenty-year-old Mercedes was unlikely to attract armed robbers - they preferred Peugeots. Sleeping alone in our large house terrified me.

To add to my pain, Maureen who had been my neighbour back in the sixties was murdered. We had been together since our children were babies and she had been my closest friend. She would never again drop in for breakfast, share jokes and chatter. We had spent many afternoons together, playing golf and table tennis. What harm could this small lady have done to anyone? The intruders first slaughtered her faithful old guard, then entered her bedroom through the hanging ceiling and broke her legs before strangling her. Her grandchildren and daughter were in the house at the time. I never knew if this was an arranged assassination or a robbery. The only way I could cope with the increasingly horrendous life in Nigeria was to concentrate on my work with Hope for the Village Child.

The quality of life was deteriorating so rapidly that our son Andrew could no longer see a future for his children and he decided to leave Kaduna. He moved to Southern Africa and the Jacaranda Restaurant was never the same again.

Eli was determined to help some of the children with rickets. During one of his visits to the Ibrahim Babangida Specialized Hospital in Minna, where he was the chairman of the board of trustees, he persuaded a surgeon to perform corrective surgery on two boys called Nehemiah and Dogara. Nehemiah's father had two wives and many children. All the offspring from his first wife had rickets, but those from his second wife had normal legs. As these children ate from the same stew pot and drank the same water, I assumed that the disease was genetic. Dogara, the youngest son of the chief of Telele, was a bright little boy, greatly hampered by his twisted knees.

The journey from Kaduna to Minna would take about three hours. Tony took the Land Rover to collect the children together with their fathers. As there was no space for us, Eli and I followed in our car. The journey was monotonous and after two hours we stopped for a break. The chief of Telele came down from the Land Rover looking very excited. I could only understand his repeated, 'Mun gode. Mun gode - Thank you. Thank you.

'What's he saying?'

Eli smiled as he interpreted. 'I never dreamed that in this life I would travel beyond Kaduna State. Now I find myself in Niger State and going to Minna. How can I tell you what this means to me? Thank you.'

The two boys understood very little about what was happening, except that they would return to their village with straight legs. I knew that they would find the sterile hospital environment, smell of disinfectant and anaesthetic strange after earthy Telele Village. I had undertaken a huge responsibility: the operation was not normally dangerous but I was aware of the risk involved with anaesthesia. My anxiety made me regret getting so deeply involved. Later Eli shared his worries with me. At the time, he was investigating a rumour that one nurse anaesthetist was demanding bribes from patients to ensure that they would wake up safely.

Two months later, a nurse lifted Dogara onto a couch, to have his grubby plaster removed. The doctor used clippers to cut through the tough casts. Overhead a fan whirled but it did not cool the hot and humid atmosphere. I stood with Dogara's father, watching the slow progress of the clippers. Occasionally the boy let out little squeaks of fear - the father held his hand firmly saying 'Ishiru' (quiet). When the casts of both legs had been cut, the nurse shelled them away. At that moment the chief let out a piercing cry that startled me. Then I understood what he was saying. 'His legs are straight. Thank you. Praise God.' I sighed with relief. This was one of the most beautiful moments of my life. The boys returned to their village able to walk normally. Months later I spotted them playing football.

Miraculously I met a wonderful orthopaedic surgeon in Kaduna called Dr Salawu. He owned a private clinic and agreed to visit the villages to see the children with rickets. Dr Salawu was shocked to witness the poverty and perplexed over the high incidence of rickets. He agreed to operate on the children if I could raise money to cover the cost of drugs, plaster and sutures. He did not charge for surgery and provided the bed and nursing-care free. I felt privileged to know this genuine man who shared my concern over the children. He was a Moslem, struggling to build a decent hospital in a failing economy. I showed many photos of children with rickets, before and after surgery, and appealed to several organisations for assistance. Almost thirty children underwent corrective surgery successfully.

Through our nurses and health-workers, I contacted many parents of affected children; we sketched family trees and marked those who in past generations had rickets. Dr Salawu and I were searching for the root cause. It appeared that the illness was passed through mothers.

One day a friend brought me some pictures of children

in India who had rickets: their unusual windswept legs strongly resembled our worst cases. Racing through the article, I searched for the cause. It had been proved that in those affected villages in India, the well water contained too much fluorine. Could this be our answer? Reading further, I noted that in both countries, the underlying rock was granite. The years I had studied geology in University doubled my excitement. If the proportion of fluorine were more than one part to a million, it could cause some genetic changes. I raced to show the article to Dr Salawu who was preparing to attend an orthopaedic conference. He took the paper along and displayed my photos. The similarities were so marked that many doctors and government officials expressed their interest. The water in Kafari, Pam Madaki and Telele needed to be tested for fluorine. Some government officials promised to act but I waited for many months and apart from a short interview, I saw no further action from the government.

As Hope for the Village Child continued to expand, my life became bogged down with administration. I would have preferred to spend more time in the villages, but to gain funding I needed to write proposals, half yearly reports and present audited accounts. The amount of office work became difficult for me to handle because I had never before used a computer. I would burn the midnight oil, struggling to type, often losing whole chunks of reports as I battled between my temperamental laptop and the fluctuating NEPA. However, I was pleased when Cafod, Manos Unidas, Van Leer, Unicef and the Tulsi Chanrai Foundation gave funding. The families working for Julius Berger donated generously and many individuals supported our cause. One lady, called Jeanne Cooper, constantly raised funds in Britain by planting flowers and arranging them in beautiful hanging baskets. It was due to Jeanne's effort and encouragement that I had persevered to build the school in Damisi. She had given us bicycles to be used as ambulances. The first day they were used, the life of a child called Mary was saved. Jeanne continues to support Mary, and her determined work for Hope for the Village Child is a source of inspiration.

On 8 June 1998 Abacha died. I was alone in the house when the news came through. There were shouts of joy in the street outside and taxis blared their horns. Officially he had suffered a heart attack, but the cause of death was uncertain. It was rumoured that he was sharing his bed with two Indian prostitutes when the 'coup from heaven' came. A few months after the dictator's death, it was reported that hundreds of millions of naira's worth of jewellery had been stolen from the Kano residence of the Abacha family; Mrs Abacha unashamedly acknowledged having purchased the jewellery on her trip to Beijing. The nation longed for an honest democratic government to give Nigerians hope for the future.

Around that time, Unicef sponsored a workshop on 'safe childbirth' for traditional birth attendants (TBAs). It had taken several weeks to persuade these women to attend. They were good-hearted, dedicated women whose methods needed polishing. The workshop was held in our large thatched chalet at the Jacaranda. Ogbaje prepared some delicious chicken groundnut stew with rice - this would please the twenty women who would have walked several miles. There were three experienced facilitators who taught the TBAs how to recognise danger signs during pregnancy and childbirth and to know when they should refer complicated cases to hospital. After the workshop, each TBA was provided with a sterile pack of scissors, gauze, cotton wool and tape for tying the cord. I felt positive that this workshop would reduce maternal deaths from infections, especially tetanus in newborns that had been so common.

Another workshop sponsored by Cafod lasted for several days. It was to train village health-workers. Our nurses worked closely with the newly selected volunteers and supplied them with basic medicines and first aid packs. They were given 'ambulance' bicycles, very useful for seeking help in emergencies. With some financial assistance from Cafod, the villagers built small health centres.

Hope for the Village Child organised many other useful workshops in the nineties. Vital topics like HIV and Aids, family spacing, child nutrition and sanitation were tackled. The workshops were popular and attendance was high because the villagers had come to realise they could improve their lives. The project was bringing great hope to the village people. When school ended, men and women would pour into the vacated classrooms, eager to begin their lessons in adult literacy.

Everything was going well until that day, 21 February 2000, when the Sharia Riots hit Kaduna. Our home was attacked and my life in Nigeria was over. Eli and I were lucky to escape because it was later said that six thousand people were slaughtered during those horrendous riots.

One interesting thing about greed is that although the underlying motive is to seek satisfaction, the irony is that even after obtaining the object of your desire you are still not satisfied.

Dalai Lama

GATWICK
23 February 2000

Our plane touched down at Gatwick in the early hours of the morning. Except for my laptop and a cabin bag, we had no other luggage. Without delay, we reached the arrivals hall where Joe was anxiously waiting. He hugged us, stood back and studied our faces, shaking his head and expressing his profound relief that we were at last safely in Britain.

It was an icy day but the sun was dazzling. The noisy traffic on the motorway sped past, aggravating my brittle nerves. Trying to keep a grip, I became silent, but my tormented brain refused to rest; the horror I had witnessed persisted in reeling through my mind, the pain increasing whenever Eli spoke of the terrible ordeal. His agonising mental torture had left him dangerously hypertensive. I reminded myself that my pain was nothing compared with his.

We stayed in Surrey for a couple of days and apart from going into Croydon for some warm clothes, fleeces and trousers, we did little else but talk about the riot, trying to make sense of what had happened.

When we felt able to face the world, we drove to our holiday home in Joe's Saab. At least we had this retreat close to the sea, where we could lick our wounds. The house was cold but I soon made it cosy.

Once the cut-off telephone lines to Kaduna had been restored, we were able to communicate with our family and friends. We had read about the riots in some of the British newspapers, but considering the thousands of people that had died, the news hardly reached the front pages.

To my great relief Tanko, our twelve-year-old foster son, was safe. He had seen the mob torching our house and fled back to school where his headmistress found him hiding with several other terrified students. She took him into her home and phoned me.

Eli's nephew Bala was less fortunate. This promising young graduate had ventured outside his compound and was fatally injured by a stray bullet.

Friends from Kaduna spoke of rumours that many non-Nigerian mercenaries had been transported into Kaduna several days before the riot. It was apparent that they came from bordering countries like Niger and Chad. It seemed that something evil had been afoot, but the Christian demonstration against Sharia law had triggered off the rioting prematurely. Christians in predominantly Moslem areas had been killed - our house was opposite a Mosque. Likewise Moslems living in strong Christian enclaves had been slaughtered. We were told of rotting corpses stacked in a heap the size of a bungalow. Whilst the Moslems had concentrated their attack on our house, hundreds of Christians in Ungwan Rimi were able to flee from the area.

A close friend phoned Eli from Minna, greatly relieved that we had reached Britain. He said that my husband's name had been mentioned in the Senate where it had been reported that he had attacked innocent Moslems as they came out of the Mosque.

Losing my cool I protested, 'What about those Moslems who were trapped in our house? Won't they speak out? Haven't they the guts to tell the truth?'

Eli was mortified. 'Where is the Ambassador to the United Arab Republic? I was treating him when we were first attacked. His windscreen was shattered when the first stones were thrown. He telephoned Peugeot and ordered a replacement. Let someone check our telephone bill - the evidence is there.' But nothing was done.

I wrote letters of gratitude to the British High

Commissioner and his wife, thanking them for their kindness. I spoke of my dismay that Eli, the victim, had now been dubbed the villain. There was no response to my letters and e-mails. I implored an acquaintance to find out why we were being snubbed by people we had considered our friends. The reply whispered over the phone was, 'They're very embarrassed.'

'Why?' I cried. 'I don't understand. Please explain. But the silence continued and Eli and I concluded that diplomats have to follow the rules - they should never become involved in internal affairs and certainly should not be seen to take sides. We reminded each other of their kindness but I felt very sad.

Later a judicial commission of enquiry was set up to investigate the Sharia Riots. I opened my laptop and wrote as Eli dictated his testimony. As he poured out the truth, his eyes streamed with tears.

We engaged a lawyer to present Eli's statement, but it seemed our testimony was submitted too late. Eventually an extension was granted and we were told that it was read.

Settling in England was not easy. I wanted to hide from most social occasions and escape from people. Whenever the subject of Kaduna was mentioned, my throat would tighten and I found it impossible to swallow. Eli, determined to make me happy, agreed that we could buy two beautiful dachshund pups. I collected them from Lincolnshire - they were very affectionate and amusing. I walked them on the beach and petted them and found I was able to laugh once again. As spring changed to summer, my mind began to heal.

We both wanted to find work but although Eli had qualified in Britain, he was considered too old to practice under the National Health Service. He accepted to go for a refresher course, but was rudely turned down; he was forced to lay his career aside. I applied for work as a teacher but at sixty-four was also considered too old. The polite man in the education department explained that I could never be insured at my age.

After a year, the Jacaranda Restaurant and Pottery were forced to close down; the staff had become slack, lacking supervision, and there was insufficient income to pay their wages. The magnificent gardens are gradually reverting to bush but I'm told that the Jacaranda trees still have purple blossom in the harmattan season and the scarlet Flame Trees light up the landscape

Ogbaje has moved to Abuja with his family. His daughter tells me he has aged and often sits in silence, staring into space.

Tanko is doing well in secondary school - he wants to be a doctor. His school reports are excellent and he will surely go to university. I heard that this special boy, whose vertebrae once stuck out 'like cotton reels', became the Junior Athletics Champion. 'Will I ever see you again?' he asks. I can only pray that I will have the means to afford his education.

Hope for the Village Child lives on. My sudden departure was premature; after I left, the project declined for a while. My greatest friend, Sister Rosa, has rescued the project. With her team, she is continuing the work, guiding the staff and striving to bring a better quality of life for the village people. The schools, wells and roving clinics continue to expand and immunisation is high on the agenda. The women are learning to sew and produce soap. This will enable them to earn some cash during the dry season. The first batch of students graduated from the Amamus schools in 2003; Dogara and a few others have moved on to secondary school.

I know that Eli will never fully recover from the shock of that attack. I remind him that God knows the full truth. Years before, when he built his hospital in Bida, he had designed a small pyramid at the entrance, the inscription read: *One World, One People, One God.* Why therefore should he become a victim of religious fanaticism?

On 18 February 2000, three days before the attack, Eli had agreed to be interviewed for a national television programme called *Meeting Point.* James Audu, who produced the programme, was an internationally renowned television producer. He was an idealist, educated in the fullest sense. He normally chose Nigerian elders for his programme, because he aimed to inspire young people by their example. It was a sunny Saturday when the television crew had appeared at our house to make the film. It portrayed Eli's life, his family, home, garden and hobbies from childhood years through to his work as a doctor. During that interview, James Audu asked Eli about his religious beliefs. Eli explained that although he was the son of a clergyman, he experienced some difficulties within the Christian religion. He found certain doctrines, namely the virgin birth and the resurrection of the body, hard to accept. He spoke of one God, emphasising that he did not believe that it was only through Jesus Christ that there would be eternal life. He reasoned that surely a God of love would accept all good people as one, regardless of their religions. He added that many of his favourite relatives were Moslem and indeed, his only daughter had married a Moslem. At the end of the day, James Audu promised to send us a copy of the film. The attack followed and we escaped from Kaduna, without the videotape.

Four days after the riots, the film was to be shown on

Nigerian National Television. Unfortunately there was a total blackout that night so it was repeated a few days later. At the end of the programme, James Audu appeared and expressed his profound dismay that our beautiful house seen in the film was now in ruins, gutted and burnt as a result of the riots.

Many friends phoned Eli in Britain to tell him that they had seen the programme. Naturally we were eager to procure the videotape because it demonstrated Eli's tolerance for all religions. There were other letters, written from different parts of Nigeria that showed that Eli had made himself unpopular with many Christians. The writers urged him to change his views and repent. We sent numerous messages to James Audu, reminding him of his promise to give Eli a copy of the videotape but apparently the film had vanished from the television archives. A few weeks later, to our utter dismay, we learnt that James Audu had tragically died in a Kaduna hospital, supposedly from asthma. We were deeply saddened.

I am thankful that none of our children were living in Nigeria when their home was destroyed. They are adults, well educated and able to fit into society anywhere in the world.

Caroline, our little poupee, is a university professor of gender studies. She lives in Africa and is married to a famous writer. She travels to many countries in the world, advocating gender balance. Their two children are rays of sunshine that brighten our lives, giving us great joy.

Andrew married an English 'rose'. They have four handsome children. Saddened at having to close the Jacaranda restaurant, Andy set to work and designed water gardens for his superb new restaurant in southern Africa. He and his wife have a flair for landscape gardening. Their two oldest boys play brilliant rugby and are in the national junior team. Their children are strong, good-looking and full of mischief.

Joe, our youngest, lives in Britain. He is a successful business consultant, full of enthusiasm for his career. His wife, also of mixed blood, is stunningly attractive. They have three healthy, sun-kissed children. We often visit them and delight in watching their strong personalities develop.

Eli and I often sit in our garden and reminisce about our lives in Nigeria. I remind him of the great work he did and the numerous lives he saved. He remembers treating the Sultan of Sokoto who regularly sent his family to Kaduna for medical treatment. We reminisce about the days when the Emirs of Zaria, Bida and Daura entrusted their lives to him when they were ill, journeying to Kaduna to see him. He also attended the family of the late Sir Kashim Ibrahim. I muse with Eli that Judi Dench was one of his most grateful patients, and he reminds me of his call-out to the Archbishop of Canterbury.

The promise that we made to each other in 1958 - that we would give our children the best of both cultures, has been fulfilled. We are proud of our children and grandchildren who fill us with joy and occasionally exhaust us.

There are many days when I remember the village children, their poverty and hunger, worlds apart from many children in the west. What of the next generation? The sheer terrorism of 'nine eleven' drew international attention; mankind was aghast at the horror; yet worse things are happening in Africa. Since 1999, over ten thousand people have been slain in Nigeria in religious riots, and five hundred thousand people are rendered homeless, too terrified to return to their roots for fear of persecution. It is sad that during that ghastly time in Nigeria, when so many people died, world reaction was only lukewarm. Does this imply that the life of an

African is of less value than that of an American or a European? What has befallen our planet that our standards are so unequal? Will there ever be peace?

It is the autumn of my life and I am in England. At night, I lie in bed and listen to the sound of the waves lapping on the beach outside my window. I reflect on my thirty-eight years in Nigeria - the thirty-eight wonderful years that Eli and I shared. I dream of the harmattan blowing through my hair; it stirs the branches of the Jacaranda trees. I am once again there, on the road to Telele. I can hear the cattle lowing in the distance; I smell the scent of wild jasmine and place my hands on the cool mud walls of the school. I hear the voices of the Jacaranda Children. I see their curly heads and their soft brown eyes, full of trust. A feeling of warmth and love lulls me to sleep. Farewell my beautiful people.

I believe that to have world peace we must first have inner peace. Those who are naturally serene, at peace with themselves, will be open towards others. I think that it is where the very foundation of universal peace lies.

Dalai Lama